LEAVE APPLICATIONS FOR JUDICIAL REVIEW

LAW AND PRACTICE

Michael A. Ntumy
Associate Professor of Law
University of Papua New Guinea

Leave Applications for Judicial Review: Law and Practice
by Michael A. Ntumy

ISBN 978-9980-945-86-0

University of Papua New Guinea Press and Bookshop
PO Box 413
University PO, NCD
Papua New Guinea

DEDICATED TO

THE MEMORY OF

THE LATE SIR BURI KIDU

(First Papua New Guinean Chief Justice)

Preface

This book, a sequel to my earlier published work entitled *Administrative Law of Papua New Guinea: Cases, Materials and Text*, was originally conceived to cover the whole field of judicial review. However, I am compelled by the exigencies of migrant labour to limit it to only the leave stage of the judicial review process. It, however, complements my earlier work by providing detailed analysis of the law and practice of judicial review.

The purpose of the book is to illustrate the application of the legal concepts, principles and doctrines of judicial review in Papua New Guinea. It seeks to bring together the court pronouncements on these legal concepts, principles and doctrines and to extract the relevant underlying law. Designed as a practical guide for legal practitioners and judges, it focuses on matters of practice and procedure which are not discussed in sufficient detail in my earlier work.

The book explains, with the aid of graphic tables and checklists, the various steps in the procedure for applying for leave to apply for judicial review, together with advice on the appropriate precedents and ways of achieving quality advocacy and judgment. In addition, it presents a complete in-depth analysis of the law and procedural mechanisms available. Since some major points of law are yet to be pronounced upon by the courts in Papua New Guinea, it is necessary to make references to decisions from other common law jurisdictions, particularly, England and Australia. Where the law is either uncertain or ill-defined by the courts, rather than state misleading dogmatic propositions, a conscientious attempt is made to highlight the consequent confusion or controversy and to draw attention to competing arguments based upon general principles. The approach adopted in doing this is expository, analytical, comparative and, at times, moderately critical. The law is stated on the basis of judgments delivered up to December 1995.

Part I of the book contains an overview of the judicial review process. It discusses the scope of the power of judicial review within the constitutional context of Papua New Guinea and indicates the type of cases that are appropriate for judicial review applications by comparing the procedure for instituting a judicial review action and that for bringing an appeal.

Part II recounts the background to the modern procedure for obtaining judicial review and explains the procedural choices available. It also features a detailed discussion of the procedure under Order 16 of the *National Court Rules*, together with a checklist to avoid pitfalls and maximise opportunities afforded by the Order. There is also a detailed discussion of the controversy about *ex parte* applications.

Part III elucidates the relevant legal principles applied by the courts in deciding on leave applications. The major principles discussed include *locus standi*, an arguable case, exhaustion of administrative remedies and undue delay. All the important decisions that have considered these principles are reviewed, with insights into how the courts apply these principles and the factors that they take into account in exercising their discretion to grant or refuse leave applications.

Part IV examines the decision-making process of the courts, accompanied by illustrative proposals on how best to apply the relevant legal principles. Finally, there is a discussion of the procedure for appealing the National Court's decision on leave and proposals for simplifying this procedure.

I am grateful to the University of Papua New Guinea for providing me with the opportunity to teach Administrative Law to the law students and, consequently, to study the system and undertake this work. I acknowledge the contribution of Mr. Brian Brunton for reviewing the draft manuscript and making helpful suggestions and critical comments; Mr. Jackson Rannells for editing the draft manuscript and proof-reading the final manuscript; Mrs. Eve Rannells, the Law Librarian, for her constant help and support; Professor Deane Arganbright for helping with the concepts for the graphic tables; and Mr. Karo Kila for introducing me to the computer software that made designing the graphic tables easy and fun. I also thank my friends and colleagues for their encouragement in completing this book. Finally, I thank my wife and children, who endured several months of inconvenience occasioned by the research and preparation of the manuscript for the book.

CONTENTS

PART IV THE DECISION ON LEAVE

Table of PNG Cases

Table of Foreign Cases

Table of Statutes

PART I

INTRODUCTION

CHAPTER 1

JUDICIAL REVIEW

Powers of the National Court

The most important and, perhaps, effective control of administrative action is the process of judicial review. This process scrutinizes the authority for an administrative agency's substantive decisions and the fairness of administrative procedure. The availability and scope of review has a direct bearing not only upon the matter under review, but also upon administrative procedures and substantive policies. The function of judicial review of administrative action is, therefore, to ensure that the administrator's action:

1. is authorized, i.e., within the delegated authority (and not *ultra vires*);
2. is fair;
3. is not an abuse of discretion, i.e., that it represents a reasonable choice supported by the available evidence;
4. does not infringe upon the freedom of the private individual, i.e., it does not encroach excessively on private individual rights.

Sources of the Power of Judicial Review

What is the source of this power of review? The power of judicial review is generally derived from either the constitution or the common law. It is, therefore, possible to distinguish two different ways in which the power of judicial review may be manifested.

The first instance, which is more aptly described as constitutional review, occurs within a constitutional framework whereby power is conferred upon the highest court of the land to declare legislative or executive action as unconstitutional. Usually, this power is conferred in order to protect personal and property rights. Judicial review, in this instance, is invariably based on a written, rigid constitution, which is changeable only through a complex amendment process. Judicial review of this type is the product of the American constitutional history, originating from the case of *Marbury v Madison*.[1] In the United States, the Supreme Court, which is vested with the power of judicial review, can adjudicate only actual cases and controversies.

The practice in Papua New Guinea reflects aspects of the American approach. According to section 18(1) of the *Constitution*, the Supreme Court has original jurisdiction, to the exclusion of other courts, as to any question relating to the interpretation or application of any provision of a Constitutional Law. The Supreme Court, therefore, has the power to rule Acts of the National Parliament as invalid or unconstitutional. In addition, the Supreme Court's interpretation of section 41 of the *Constitution* buttresses the Court's power of judicial review.[2] Unlike the Supreme Court in the United States, however, the Supreme Court of Papua New Guinea can exercise this power in the form of an advisory opinion.[3]

The second form in which the power of judicial review may be manifested is statutory interpretation and review of the decisions of administrative bodies and inferior tribunals. That is to say, the courts, while professing to be interpreting the decision, may put on the decision a wider or more restrictive meaning, using the common law techniques of statutory interpretation. This, however, has a more limited scope than constitutional review. Indeed, even though the courts frequently engage in statutory interpretation that may have the ultimate effect of reviewing legislation, in theory, in the absence of a constitutional grant of the power of judicial review, the courts normally limit their power of review to the decisions of administrative bodies and inferior tribunals.

The courts in Papua New Guinea also have the power to review administrative action in this latter sense. Section 155(3) of the *Constitution* is explicit in that, subject to the overriding jurisdiction of Supreme Court, the National Court has inherent power to review any exercise of judicial authority. A fundamental requirement of the exercise

[1] (1803) 1 Cranch 137 (USSC).
[2] See *Raz v Matane* [1986] PNGLR 38.
[3] See *SCR No 4 of 1980; Re Petition of Somare* [1981] PNGLR 265.

of this power is that the matter to be reviewed must relate to the exercise of judicial authority by an inferior tribunal or court. For example, where an inferior court, a statutory body or a domestic tribunal exercises its power to deprive a person of public or private rights.

Section 155(4) of the *Constitution* bestows on both the Supreme Court and the National Court "inherent power to make, in such circumstances as seem to them proper, orders in the nature of prerogative writs and such other orders as are necessary to do justice in the circumstances of a particular case".[4]

Cases Appropriate for Judicial Review

In principle, judicial review is concerned only with the protection of rights under public law. Consequently, the nature of the persons and bodies against whom relief may be granted in judicial review proceedings is usually limited to statutory bodies and other bodies created and regulated by public law. For this reason, actions involving the private rights and duties of parties that arise under contract, property or tort are generally not subject to judicial review.[5] The main factor that determines whether a matter is one of public law or private law is the formal source of the particular power that is being exercised, and not the status of the body exercising the power. Hence, a contract between a statutory body (e.g. a university) and its employees is not subject to the judicial review process since, although the university is a creature of public law, its contractual power is wholly derived from the law of contract, which is not public law.[6]

---

[4] See also Sch 2.2(1) and (2) of the *Constitution*, which relate to the adoption of the rules and principles of the common law, equity and the Royal Prerogative as they existed in England immediately before Papua New Guinea gained independence.

[5] Ref. *Sulaiman v PNG University of Technology* (1987) N610; *Air Niugini v Joel* [1992] PNGLR 132.

[6] See *Kuluah v University of PNG* [1993] PNGLR 494. See also *Wedau v Daniel* [1995] PNGLR 357; SC 489 where the Supreme Court held that the position of the appellant and the nature of his work as legal officer of the PNG Habours Board did not place him in a "public office" as contemplated by the *PNG Harbours Board Ordinance 1963-1969*. Consequently, any rights that he may have as an employee of the Board are contractual, based upon private law. As such, a matter concerning his employment was not susceptible to judicial review.

However, on account of the absence of a general theory of "public law" in English law, it is not unusual to see some of the substantive principles of judicial review being applied to private bodies such as the committees of clubs, universities, trade union organizations and other voluntary organizations. While the decision to extend the judicial review procedure to such bodies is often made on an *ad hoc* basis, the common factor in all such decisions is that the bodies must be in a position to exercise power relating to matters of public concern or must be exercising "judicial authority", i.e. functions of a disciplinary or similar nature which entail depriving a person of private or public rights.

Non-reviewable Decisions (Ouster Clauses)

In reviewing administrative action or inaction, one of the major threshold questions is whether the particular court before which the matter is brought has jurisdiction to review the case or not. The consideration of this issue assumes importance, particularly, in situations where there are constitutional implications, such as the interpretation and application of the provisions of the *Constitution.* Aside from this issue, there is also the preliminary question of whether the reviewing court has power to review the particular subject matter or whether the action is committed to the administrative authority's discretion? In other words, what actions of an administrative authority are reviewable? The significance of this question is heightened by the occasional attempts by the legislature to exclude the power of the courts to review certain administrative actions.

Certain statutes, having established an appeal or review procedure, assert that the decision of the appellate or reviewing body is final or is not subject to further appeal to any court. Even on statutory appeal or review, jurisdictional defects, allegations of bias, failure to give notice of the proceedings, errors on the fact of the record are all matters which can bring the appellate or reviewing body's own decision into disrepute. In that event, the complainant with a legitimate grievance at first instance will have been twice exposed to defective decision-making processes.

The common law position during the 19th century on the question of reviewability was that administrative action was usually unreviewable in the absence of legislative intent to permit review. The law has since changed. The 20th century position has shifted from a presumption of unreviewability to a presumption of reviewability. In other words, there is a general presumption against ousting the jurisdiction of the courts, so that even the silence of the legislature on the issue is not to be construed as indicating a legislative intent to preclude review. Hence, statutory provisions which purport to exclude judicial review, whether coupled with an alternative statutory remedy or not, are construed restrictively. This means that if there is more than one way in which the provisions can reasonably be construed, the construction that least impairs the jurisdiction of the courts will be selected.[7]

For example, a clause which states that a decision shall be "final" is not construed as excluding judicial review. On the contrary, such a clause merely excludes any right of appeal that would otherwise exist[8] and also prevents the decision-making body from revoking its own decisions.[9] Similarly, a clause that states that a "decision shall not be questioned in any court of law" is construed to apply to only legally valid decisions. The courts will, therefore, conduct an initial enquiry to determine the legal validity of the decision. If the purported decision is *ultra vires* and void, then since it does not count as a "decision" in law, it is presumed that the ouster clause does not apply.[10]

Although the current practice in Papua New Guinea follows the position of the law in England very closely, the legal basis for it is constitutional.[11] A summary of the practice in Papua New Guinea may be stated in the following general terms. The courts generally review administrative action except where:

---

[7] Ref. *Pearlman v Keepers and Governors of Harrow School* [1979] QB 56; [1978] 3 WLR 736; [1979] 1 All ER 365.

[8] Ref. *Tehrani v Rostron* [1972] 1 QB 182; [1971] 3 All ER 790; [1971] 3 WLR 612.

[9] Ref. *Punton v Ministry of Pensions and National Insurance (No 2)* [1964] 1 All ER 448, [1964] 1 WLR 226.

[10] Ref. *Anisminic Ltd v Foreign Compensation Commission* [1969] 2 AC 147; [1969] 1 All ER 208; [1969] 2 WLR 163.

[11] Ref. section 155 of the *Constitution*, which gives the courts inherent power to consider any question relating to the interpretation or application of any law.

1. the power of review is removed or restricted by a Constitutional Law or an Act of Parliament.[12]
2. the enabling statute reveals a precise intent against review, i.e., statutory exclusion of judicial review.[13]
3. the question presented is not suitable or appropriate for judicial determination.[14]
4. some special reason, e.g. availability of an alternative method of challenge such as a statutory right of appeal, which makes review undesirable.[15]

Generally, however, even where a statute or subordinate legislation purports to oust the jurisdiction of the courts, the courts will nevertheless inquire into the matter in order to determine the constitutionality of the statute.[16] So also, where the courts regard themselves as incompetent to review a case because the subject matter of the case is unsuitable or inappropriate for review, they will still conduct an initial enquiry in order

---

[12] Section 155(2)(e) of the *Constitution*.

[13] E.g. *Premdas v PNG* [1979] PNGLR 329; *SCR No 5 of 1985;* Re *Raz v Matane* [1985] PNGLR 329; *Raz v Matane* [1986] PNGLR 38; *Evaisa v Hela* OS 247/92; *Busu v PTC* [1993] PNGLR 321; *Valentine v Somare* [1988-89] PNGLR 51. Ref. section 155(3)(e) of the *Constitution*, which permits the removal or restriction of the powers of judicial review by a Constitutional Law or a statute. Ref. also the constitutional provisions which are non-justiciable, and the discussion of these in *Wari v Ramoi* [1986] PNGLR 112.

[14] E.g. matters concerning national security or legislative powers of Parliament. See *Mininga v Culligan* [1995] PNGLR 387; (1995) N1348 where the National Court dismissed an application for judicial review because only Parliament, and not the courts, had power to add categories prescribed in a legislation. The Court, therefore, advised that the matter was better resolved by reference to the Secretary of Personnel Management.

[15] E.g. *Sulaiman v PNG University of Technology*, above, note 5.

[16] See *Re Moresby North East Election Petition* [1977] PNGLR 429 where, even though section 220 of the *Organic Law on National Elections* provided that "a decision of the National Court is final and conclusive and without appeal, and shall not be questioned in any way", the Supreme Court reviewed the legislation and held that it was invalid to the extent that it purported to exclude the Supreme Court's inherent discretionary power under section 155(2)(b) of the *Constitution* to review all judicial acts of the National Court. See also *Ombudsman Commission v Donohoe* [1985] PNGLR 348 where, notwithstanding section 24 of the *Organic Law on the Ombudsman Commission*, which clearly provided that "no proceeding of the Commission ... shall be challenged, reviewed, quashed or called into question in any court", the Supreme Court, nonetheless, reviewed the legislation and found it to be inconsistent with section 217(6) of the *Constitution*. See also section 155(5) of the *Constitution*, which permits the National Court to review cases in spite of ouster clauses if there are "over-riding considerations of public policy in the special circumstances of a particular case." Ref. *Mase v PNG* (1980) N260.

to establish the *bona fides* of the government's claim that the matter is unsuitable or inappropriate for review.

Distinction Between an Appeal and Judicial Review

Under the *Constitution*, the Supreme Court and the National Court both have appellate as well as review jurisdictions. The Supreme Court, as the final court of appeal, has an appellate jurisdiction to hear appeals from the National Court and an inherent power to review all judicial acts of the National Court.[17] The National Court also has an inherent power to review any exercise of judicial authority[18] and, as a superior court of record, has an unlimited jurisdiction to hear appeals from the Local Courts and the District Courts.[19]

While the National Court has jurisdiction under the *Constitution* to hear appeals from the Local Courts and the District Courts, the right of appeal is a statutory right. In many cases, statutory rights of appeal lie to the National Court against decisions of the Local Courts and the District Courts as well as the decisions of administrative authorities which, in the performance of their duties, exercise judicial authority. The most common remedy in cases where a person is aggrieved by the decision of a public authority or tribunal is, therefore, the right of an appeal from the decision or determination. However, that right can, as a matter of law, only be conferred by the legislation relating to the statutory authority concerned. It is a well established principle of law that the right of appeal to a court or other appellate body is the creature of statute.

In many instances, appeals from what are essentially "administrative" decisions are diverted away from the courts in favour of tribunals specially created by statute to review the basis of the complainant's grievance. The right of appeal to the National Court should, therefore, be distinguished from cases where alternative methods of challenge are provided, for example, a statutory right of appeal to an administrative authority. In such cases, the challenge against the decision of an

[17] Section 155(2)(a) and (b) of the *Constitution*.
[18] Section 155(3)(a) of the *Constitution*.
[19] Sections section 219 of Part XI of the *District Courts Act* (Ch 40) and section 43(2) of the *Local Courts Act* (Ch 41).

administrative authority may lie to a higher administrative body, tribunal, or to a government minister. This latter type of appeal is referred to as an alternative remedy (as opposed to judicial remedies).

Although the procedures of the two processes are similar in some respects, there are fundamental differences. Since both types of appeal depend entirely on particular statutes, the nature and extent of the statutory right of appeal, the procedure to be followed, the time limits to be obeyed and the basis on which the appellate body can act are all determined by the particular legislation in question. In both appeal proceedings, the original decision is open to full reconsideration, and the appellate body may substitute its own decision on the substantive issue for that of the original body.[20] However, in accordance with the hierarchies of tribunals, from administrative to judicial, since the statutory appeals body is an administrative tribunal, its decision is subject to the appellate and/or review jurisdictions of the National Court. On the contrary, the National Court's decision on appeal, unless appealed to the Supreme Court, is final.

The procedure on appeal to the National Court is governed by Order 18 of the *National Court Rules* (Ch 38), Part XI of the *District Courts Act* (Ch 40) and section 43(2) of the *Local Courts Act* (Ch 41). The main features of the appeal procedure may be summarised as follows:

1. An appeal to the National Court depends entirely upon the above statutes.[21]
2. Leave to appeal is not required.
3. The appeal is by way of re-hearing and is instituted by notice of appeal and by entering into a recognizance on appeal, or by giving other specified security.
4. The time limit for instituting the appeal is within 30 days of the date of the decision being appealed against.
5. All parties to the appeal must be appear or be represented at the hearing.

---

[20] For a detailed discussion of the statutory appeals procedure, see *De Smith's Judicial Review of Administrative Action* 4th edn by J M Evans (ed) (London: Sweet & Maxwell 1980) ch 6.

[21] Ref. above, note 19.

6. On the hearing of the appeal, the Court may *prima facie* affirm, quash or vary the conviction, order or adjudication appealed from, or substitute its own decision for that of the body appealed against, or remit the case for further hearing by the Court which made the conviction, order or adjudication or by any other competent court.

The right to appeal may be limited by many situations. For example, where a person aggrieved by a decision of a statutory authority or person exercising statutory power has no specific right of appeal. This occurs where the relevant legislation has made no provision for an appropriate appeal procedure. Even where provision is made for the right of appeal to an administrative authority, the relevant provision may purport to oust the jurisdiction of the courts, thereby precluding any recourse to the courts. In all these situations, judicial review would be still be available to challenge the decision.

Judicial review is the power of the superior courts to control, by way of supervision, the exercise of judicial authority by inferior courts or tribunals. In Papua New Guinea, this is an entirely separate procedure which is firmly entrenched by the *Constitution*. Subject to certain constitutional and statutory restraints, judicial review is not limited to the supervisory control of the lower courts by the superior courts. Judicial review also extends to all manner of tribunals and other bodies discharging public (and, in some circumstances, private) duties. The procedure for instituting judicial review proceedings is contained in the Order 16 of the *National Court Rules* (Ch 38), which is fully discussed in Chapter 4 below.

An application for judicial review is not an appeal; neither is it an alternative to an appeal. In theory and in practice, there is a clear distinction between them which is now well established in law. The main principles[22] governing the exercise of the judicial review jurisdiction which distinguish it from an appeal are as follows:

---

[22] These principles are derived from *R v Chief Constable; ex parte Calveley* [1986] 1 QB 424; [1986] 1 ALL ER 257; [1986] 2 WLR 144. They were subsequently adopted by the Supreme Court in *PNG v Kapal* [1987] PNGLR 417 and applied in *Kekedo v Burns Philp (PNG) Ltd* [1988-89] PNGLR 122.

1. The judicial review jurisdiction of the National Court is discretionary.
2. The purpose of judicial review is not to examine the reasoning of the subordinate authority with a view to substituting the court's opinion. Judicial review is concerned with the decision-making process, not with the decision.
3. The circumstances under which judicial review may be available are where the decision-making authority exceeds its powers, commits an error of law, commits a breach of natural justice, reaches a decision which no reasonable tribunal could have reached or abuses its powers.[23]
4. In cases where a right of appeal to the National Court lies against the decisions of inferior courts or tribunals, the question as to whether or not the existence of a right of appeal excludes the right to invoke the review jurisdiction of the National Court is a matter for the Court's discretion, depending upon whether it is the decision or the decision-making process that is being challenged.
5. Even in cases where no appeal lies against an order or a decision, judicial review would, nevertheless, be still available to challenge the validity or reasonableness of the order or decision. This jurisdiction can only be taken away by express provision.[24]
6. The judicial review jurisdiction of the National Court exists even where statutory appeal procedures are provided by Parliament.
7. Save in the most exceptional circumstances, the rule is that the judicial review jurisdiction will not be

---

[23] Unless one of these specific grounds is established, judicial review may not be available. See *Kaupa v Register of Workers Compensation* (1995) N1300 where the National Court held that in the absence of any of these grounds, an allegation that a tribunal's decision was "harsh and oppressive" was not a valid ground upon which an application for judicial review may be based.
[24] Ref. *Ombudsman Commission v Donohoe*, above, note 16.

exercised by the National Court where alternative remedies, such as statutory appeal procedure, are available.

8. Whether the statutory appeal procedure would be quicker or slower than the procedure by way of judicial review; whether the matter depends on some particular or technical knowledge which is more readily available to the statutory appeal body are among the matters which the Court may take into account when considering the exercise of discretion. The fact that judicial review is quicker and more convenient is, of itself, not sufficient ground for the exercise of the judicial review jurisdiction.

PART II

THE LEAVE PROCEDURE

CHAPTER 2

APPLICATION FOR LEAVE

Background to the Modern Procedure

Before the *National Court Rules* (Ch 38) came into effect, the procedure for obtaining judicial review was based upon the common law rules of procedure. This procedure allowed applicants to bring action by writ or originating summons claiming relief similar in effect to the prerogative orders of prohibition, *certiorari* and *mandamus*. It was not possible to seek an injuction, declaration or damages. There was no provision for discovery or interrogatories, and there was no express provision for cross-examination of deponents upon evidence contained in affidavits, nor was such cross-examination in practice ordered. These and other insurmountable hurdles rendered the judicial review process an inadequate remedy in many cases.

The *National Court Rules* (Ch 38) came into effect on 4 July 1983. Order 16 of the Rules replaced the previous cumbersome procedure for applying for the prerogative writs, which can now be obtained through a single, unified procedure called "an application for judicial review". This development followed the change introduced by Order 53 of the *Rules of the Supreme Court* (U.K.), which in 1977 provided a comprehensive code of procedure and a single application for judicial review. The procedure for applying for judicial review under Order 16 is, thus, considerably simplified and standardised.

Under the changes introduced by Order 16, an applicant is permitted to combine a claim for injunctions, declarations and even damages with a claim for a prerogative order. There is express provision for discovery, interrogatories and cross-examination.

The procedure for obtaining judicial review of administrative action is outlined in the *National Court Rules* (Ch 38). The principal form of this procedure is an application for judicial review under Order 16 of the *National Court Rules* (Ch 38) for:

1. an order of judicial review in the nature of the former prerogative writs of *certiorari*, prohibition,

mandamus and *quo warranto*; and, subject to certain restrictive conditions,

2. an injunction; and
3. a declaration.

There are other forms, such as an application by originating process under Order 4 of the Rules for an injunction and a declaration[1] and an application under Order 17 of the Rules for a writ of *habeas corpus*. This would seem to give an applicant the option to proceed by Order 16 or by ordinary action. Because of the constitutional implications, in practice, the ordinary action is accepted as a normal method of reviewing administrative decisions. The procedural accuracy of this method and the judicial position on the issue is discussed in detail in Chapter 3 below.

The new procedure, however, requires that an application for judicial review must be preceded by an application for leave to apply for judicial review. If and only if leave is granted by the National Court does the matter then proceed to the substantive hearing. In practice, this means that the determination as to whether an administrative decision should be subject to review or not goes through two stages. The first stage is a preliminary stage during which the National Court, without delving into the substantive issues of the case, determines whether to permit the applicant to challenge the administrative decision or not. In other words, the court exercises its discretion to grant or refuse leave for the applicant to challenge the administrative decision. It is only when leave is granted that the case may proceed to the second stage, during which the court hears arguments on the substantive issues of the case and reviews the legality and merits of the administrative decision.

The determination to grant or refuse leave to apply for judicial review is based upon four major legal principles:

1. **"Standing" / *Locus standi*** involves the question of whether the applicant has "sufficient interest" in the matter to bring an action in court.

[1] The courts have, however, overruled this Order as an inappropriate form for applying for judicial review. See *Masive v Okuk* [1985] PNGLR 105 and *B Fortunaso Pty Ltd v Bank of South Pacific Ltd* [1992] PNGLR 275.

2. **An arguable case** involves the question of whether the application raises any fundamental or serious legal issues.
3. **Exhaustion of administrative remedies** raises the question of whether a party should be required to pursue further administrative appeal before bringing the matter to court.
4. **Delay** involves the question of whether the application is brought within the prescribed, or otherwise reasonable, time.

These legal principles are discussed in detail in Part III below.

Purpose and Function of Leave

The principal purpose of the requirement for leave is to enable the courts to screen all applications for judicial review, filter them and then select those cases which are considered appropriate for, or worthy of, review. This filtering process serves many purposes and functions.

First, it is meant to provide a quick method of sifting out hopeless applications. The objective is to provide the courts with the opportunity to screen and select cases that merit judicial review in order to safeguard against the courts being flooded with unmeritorious cases. The rationale for this is to ensure that "the time of the court ... [is not] ... wasted by busybodies with misguided or trivial complaints of administrative error, and to remove the uncertainty in which public officers and authorities might be left whether they could safely proceed with administrative action while proceedings for judicial review of it were actually pending even though misconceived."[2] Accordingly, the requirement for leave restricts interference with the policy and administrative decisions of public officials to situations where the applicant has a "sufficient interest" or "standing" in the matter.

---

[2] Per Lord Diplock, in *Inland Revenue Commissioners v National Federation of Self- Employed and Small Businesses Ltd* [1981] 2 All ER 93 at 105; [1982] AC 617 at 643; [1981] 2 WLR 722 at 739.

The second objective of the leave requirement is to enable the courts to regulate the timing of judicial review applications. This function of the leave filter may be viewed from two angles.

On the one hand, an application for leave may be premature, in the sense that the case is not yet "ripe" for judicial determination. For instance, a suit may be brought to challenge a decision or an order which is still subject to change, at the request of the applicant, by the highest authority within the administrative organization. In such a case, since the applicant still has an opportunity to have the grievance redressed administratively, it is required, as a cost and time-saving measure, that this option must first be exhausted before proceeding to court. Otherwise, on the ground that the applicant has not exhausted all the available administrative remedies, the courts are likely to refuse to grant leave to the applicant. This ensures that the courts' time will not be occupied with frivolous or nuisance suits. The doctrinal basis of this ground - exhaustion of administrative remedies - is discussed in detail in Chapter 10 below.

On the other hand, an application which is instituted too late, that is, after the decision being challenged has been made, may become barred by delay if the circumstances suggest that the delay is unreasonable. Hence, for example, if applicants sit on their rights for an unreasonable time before attempting to assert them through the judicial review process, the courts have the discretion to refuse leave on the grounds of "undue delay".

The leave hurdle also operates as a cost-saving measure to ensure that the judicial review process is not unduly expensive. The fact that leave is required as a prerequisite for applying for judicial review makes it possible to filter out applications of cranks and busybodies who might otherwise impose excessive financial burden on the process of legitimate administration. This objective is achieved by requiring that applications for leave to apply for judicial review are made *ex parte*, so that the proposed respondents to any application who do not need to be represented are not unnecessarily inconvenienced or subjected to unnecessary expense at this early stage.

Finally, since the grant or refusal of leave depends entirely on the discretion of the court, the leave requirement also gives the court the opportunity to control applications of its motion, for example, by refusing leave or permitting them to proceed only in such manner as it may direct.

CHAPTER 3

CHOICE OF PROCEDURE

Procedures for Obtaining Judicial Review

Section 155(4) of the *Constitution* bestows on both the Supreme Court and the National Court "inherent power to make, in such circumstances as seem to them proper, orders in the nature of prerogative writs and such other orders as are necessary to do justice in the circumstances of a particular case".[1] Section 23(2) of the *Constitution* provides that: "Where a provision of a Constitutional Law prohibits or restricts an act or imposes a duty, the National Court may, if it thinks it proper to do so, make any order that it thinks proper for preventing or remedying a breach of the prohibition, restriction or duty ..."

Since the *Constitution* does not restrict the exercise of the above powers to any exclusive procedure, this means that, in principle, it is possible to seek and obtain judicial review of administrative decisions outside the procedure set out in Order 16 of the *National Court Rules* (Ch 38). In practice, this has been done by seeking declaratory and injunctive relief by ordinary action by writ or by ordinary originating summons pursuant to sections 155(4) and 23(2) of the *Constitution*.[2]

---

[1] See also Sch 2.2(1) and (2) of the *Constitution*, which relate to the adoption of the rules and principles of the common law, equity and the Royal Prerogative as they existed in England immediately before Papua New Guinea gained independence.

[2] Some litigants have attempted to institute judicial review proceedings pursuant to Order 4 and 5 of the *National Court Rules*. The courts have, however, overruled these Orders as inappropriate forms for applying for judicial review. In *Masive v Okuk* [1985] PNGLR 105, the plaintiff commenced the proceedings by way of originating summons pursuant to Order 4 of the *National Court Rules*, seeking a declaration. The Court dismissed the application because it was not supported by an affidavit of facts. In the Court's view, the Order 4 procedure should only be used where the facts are not in dispute. In *B Fortunaso Pty Ltd v Bank of South Pacific Ltd* [1992] PNGLR 275, the plaintiff commenced action by motion on originating summons, seeking declaratory relief as well interlocutory injunctive orders. Although the application was supported by an affidavit, there were no pleadings. Brown J struck out the application because it did not comply with Order 4 Rule 7 of the *National Court Rules*, which requires that originating summons should be accompanied by a statement of claim which shows a cause of action upon which the Court's jurisdiction would be based. According to the Court, while the National Court

The use of the *Constitution* as an alternative means of instituting an application for leave to apply for judicial review was upheld by the Supreme Court in *PNG v Sisia.*[3] The Court held in this case that section 23(2) of the *Constitution* -

> ...would empower the court to make an order quashing the Minister's declaration of December 1979 or declaring it invalid which is exactly the kind of order which could have been obtained under s 155(4). In other words, the trial judge's declaration invalidating the Minister's declaration could have been made under s 23(2) or s 155(4).[4]

Similarly, in *NCDIC v Bogibada Holdings Pty Ltd,*[5] it was held that "The National Court has power to make merely declaratory orders according to the principles adopted under Sch 2.2 of the *Constitution*, such powers deriving from s 155(4) of the *Constitution*."[6]

The fact that applications for leave to apply for judicial review that are brought under these two sections of the *Constitution* invariably require that the applicant must first obtain leave of the court before the application can be heard is not in dispute. However, since these constitutional provisions merely confer the power to make certain orders without prescribing the procedure by which the power may be invoked, this raises the question as to the relevant practice and procedure that is applicable to proceedings to enforce the constitutional provisions. The current practice in this regard indicates that the procedure adopted to enforce the constitutional provisions may vary depending upon which section of the *Constitution* is involved.

For instance, in *PNG v Sisia,* the Court fashioned out an *ad hoc* procedure which required that to seek relief under sections 23(2) and 155(4) of the *Constitution*, the applicant must satisfy the Court that there has not been unreasonable delay by in bringing the action. Incidentally, the Court relied on the principle of undue delay as it applies under Order 16 Rule 4 of the *National Court Rules* as a guide. It did so, however, not because it considered that this was required by the Order 16 procedure but only to assist the Court in interpreting "unreasonable delay". In

---

has the power under section 155(4) of the *Constitution* to make declaratory orders, it must have jurisdiction to entertain the action.

[3] [1987] PNGLR 102.

[4] *Id.*, p. 112.

[5] [1987] PNGLR 135.

[6] *Ibid.* See also *Lowa v Akipe* [1992] PNGLR 399.

NCDIC v Bogibada Holdings Pty Ltd, the Court adopted its own procedure, which required that to seek relief under section 155(4) of the *Constitution*, it is necessary for the applicants to have *locus standi*. Although this requirement was determined by reference to the sufficient interest test laid down in Order 16 of the *National Court Rules,*[7] again the Court did not feel bound to apply the test nor did it apply it because it was required under Order 16. Clearly, the Court in this instance, just as in the previous case, was compelled to rely on Order 16 principles because of the absence of any established principles guiding how applications brought under sections 23(2) and 155(4) of the *Constitution* should be considered. Finally, in *B Fortunaso Pty Ltd v Bank of South Pacific Ltd,*[8] an entirely different procedure was adopted whose only requirement was that, to seek relief under section 155(4) of the *Constitution*, there must be a dispute between the parties.[9]

The holdings in these cases show that the procedure adopted in applications for leave to apply for judicial review that are brought under the *Constitution* have varied substantially from that prescribed under Order 16 of the *National Court Rules*. The resulting multiplicity of procedures for invoking the judicial review jurisdiction of the National Court raises the question as to whether a choice of procedures is permitted. If not, then is the Order 16 procedure an exclusive procedure for bringing an application for judicial review?

---

[7] See *Ponda v Mamun Investments Pty Ltd* [1991] PNGLR 337.

[8] *B Fortunaso*, above, note 2.

[9] Cf. *PNG v Colbert* [1988] PNGLR 138, where the Supreme Court entertained an application for judicial review pursuant to s 155(2)(b) of the *Constitution*. In the absence any established procedure for bringing an application under this section of the *Constitution*, the Supreme Court resorted to an ad hoc procedure. It held that an application under this section must be brought within the time limit stipulated in the *Supreme Court Act* (Ch 37) s 17 for filing notice of appeal, otherwise the discretionary power to grant such a review should be exercised only where (1) it is in the interests of justice; (2) there are cogent and convincing reasons and exceptional circumstances, where some substantial injustice is manifest or the case is of special gravity; and (3) there are clear legal grounds meriting a review of the decision. See also *Donigi v Base Resources Ltd* [1992] PNGLR 110.

Procedural Choices

The National Court has considered this question on a number of occasions. In *Masive v Okuk*,[10] the plaintiff commenced proceedings by way of originating summons pursuant to the *National Court Rules*, Order 4, for a declaration concerning the residency of a nominated candidate for election. The summons also sought an injunction to restrain the electoral officers from placing the nominated candidate's name on the electoral papers. Pratt J dismissed the application on the basis of not complying with the rule that applications by way of originating summons under Order 4 of the *National Court Rules* should be accompanied by an affidavit of facts. In an *obiter*, the Court also considered the issue as to whether or not Order 4 was the appropriate procedure by which to challenge or affect the actions of a public officer in the course of his duties. On this point, Pratt J expressed the following view:

> ... I tend to the view that the procedure by way of O 16 for a declaration and injunction is the more appropriate method in a case such as the present where a party wishes to challenge or affect the actions of a public officer in the course of his duties. In short, the present application under O 4 is misconceived and should have been brought under O 16, r 2, by way of judicial review. I adopt a statement by Lord Diplock in *O'Reilly v. Mackman* [1982] 3 WLR 1096, referred to me by Mr. Colquhoun-Kerr, (at 110, par c) where his Lordship says:
>
> > 'Now that those disadvantages to applicants have been removed and all remedies for infringements of rights protected by public law can be obtained upon an application for judicial review, as can also remedies for infringements of rights under private law if such infringements should also be involved, it would in my view as a general rule be contrary to public policy, and as such an abuse of the process of the court, to permit a person seeking to establish that a decision of a public authority infringed rights to which he was entitled to protection under public law to proceed by way of an ordinary action and by this means to evade the provisions of O 53 for the protection of such authorities.'[11]

Perhaps because Pratt J's opinion is not binding, there have been many instances where the courts have entertained applications to challenge or affect the actions of public officers in the course of their duties under

---

[10] Above, note 2.

[11] *Id.*, pp. 106-107. See also *Malapu v Electoral Commission* [1987] PNGLR 128 and *PNG Coffee Industry Board v Panga Coffee Factory Ltd* [1990] PNGLR 363.

procedures other than that prescribed under Order 16. In *NCDIC v Bogibada Holdings Pty Ltd*,[12] while considering the desirability or undesirability of multiplicity of proceedings for instituting judicial review applications, Kapi DCJ indicated that an application for judicial review may be brought under either Order 16 or section 155(4) of the *Constitution*. In *Guggemos v Acting Minister of Foreign Affairs*,[13] Amet J (as he then was) entertained an application for judicial review brought under section 155(4) of the *Constitution* without addressing his mind to the issue. In this case, the plaintiff applied to challenge the decision of the Minister for Foreign Affairs to cancel his entry permit and to order his removal from the country.

Recently, the issue came up in the Supreme Court case of *National Executive Council v Public Employees Association of Papua New Guinea*.[14] This was an appeal against the decision of the National Court declaring the appointment of Luke Lucas (the third appellant) as the Secretary and Departmental Head of the Department of Attorney-General illegal and, therefore, null and void *ab initio*. On appeal, counsel for the first and second appellants argued that the originating summons by which the case was instituted in the National Court was an abuse of process of the court in that the matter should have proceeded by way of judicial review under Order 16 of the *National Court Rules*.

Rejecting this argument, the Supreme Court ruled that there is no absolute rule that obliges the proceedings to have commenced by way of the procedure prescribed under Order 16, even if it was seen to be more appropriate. This view was supported by Lord Diplock's comments in *O'Reilly v Mackman*[15] on changes introduced by Order 53 in the UK, in which he said *inter alia*:

> My Lords, Order 53 does not expressly provide that procedure by application for judicial review shall be the exclusive procedure available by which the remedy of a declaration or injunction may be obtained for infringement of rights that are entitled to protection under public law...[16]

[12] Above, note 5.
[13] [1987] PNGLR 352.
[14] [1993] PNGLR 264.
[15] [1982] 3 WLR 1096; [1983] 2 AC 237; [1982] 3 All ER 1124.
[16] *Id.*, at pp. 1109, 284, and 1134 respectively; note 14 at 267.

Declaring this as analogous to the situation under Order 16, the Supreme Court held that it is open to an applicant to choose any of the procedures under the Rules. As to what may amount to an abuse of process, the Court rejected the rule in *O'Reilly v Mackman* that failure to use the Order 16 procedure would be an abuse of process, since that procedure has been specifically provided for the pursuit of private rights in public law. The Court distinguished the position in Papua New Guinea as follows:

> Order 16 does not make any distinction between declarations or injunctions as a remedy for infringement of a right protected under public law as opposed to those under private law. The distinctions in O 16 relate to the nature of remedies set out in r 1(1), which provides judicial review as the exclusive procedure, and declaration or injunction under r 1(2) which provides for optional procedures.
>
> An abuse of the process of the court may arise where, in an application for a remedy under O 16 r 1(1), a party can also obtain a declaration or injunction but does not do so and, subsequently, applies to obtain such an order by way of writ or originating summons in a separate proceeding. That would be an attempt to avoid the requirements under O 16 and would, as well, constitute multiplicity of proceedings. It is not wise to indicate the circumstances that may amount to an abuse of the process of the court. This can be developed on a case by case basis.[17]

Since the respondent in this case applied for only a declaration and had not applied for a remedy under Order 16 Rule 1, the Court found that there was no abuse of process.[18] In so holding, the Court emphasized that the determination of the question as to whether the choice of procedure is an abuse of process or not is a discretionary one, and the Court may exercise its discretion to direct the more appropriate procedure.[19]

---

[17] Above, note 14 at 268.

[18] The issue arose again in *Haiveta v Wingti* [1994] PNGLR 160. The Court, following the Supreme Court ruling on the issue, held at p. 166 that "notwithstanding that it may be argued that this application might have been more appropriately brought by way of application for judicial review [under Order 16], application by originating process is not obviously inappropriate."

[19] Cf. *Novau v Mark* [1992] PNGLR 229. In this case, the plaintiff, having obtained leave to apply for judicial review, proceeded by ordinary notice of motion to seek judicial review of the decision of the Electoral Commission not to permit him to nominate for the Alotau Seat after the expiration of the statutory period for nominations. Sakora AJ, after noting the confusion caused by bringing the action as an ordinary notice of motion and the absence of the order granting leave on the file, exercised his discretion under Order 1 Rule 7 of the *National Court Rules* to convert the action from the originally intended application for judicial review and treated the application as if it had been commenced by an ordinary notice of motion. In his view, it would not have been proper, under the

On the authority of this Supreme Court decision, it is indisputably clear that the current position of the law is that the Order 16 procedure is not an exclusive procedure for bringing an application for judicial review, and a choice of procedures is permitted. This position of the law may be viewed from two diametrically opposed angles. On the one hand, the position is commendable in the name of justice and is in complete agreement with the profound statement made by Collins MR in *Re Coles and Ravenshear*[20] and cited with approval by Wilson J[21] and Sakora AJ.[22] The statement reads thus:

> Although I agree that a Court cannot conduct its business without a code of procedure, I think that the relation of rules of practice to the work of justice is intended to be that of handmaiden rather than mistress, and the court ought not to be so far bound and tied by rules, which are after all only intended as general rules of procedure, as to be compelled to do what will cause injustice in the particular case.[23]

A similar sentiment was expressed by Chief Justice Napier of the South Australian Supreme Court in the case of *Blight v Warman and McAllan*,[24] where he said:

> But, however that may be, the practice of the Court is the law of the Court and, according to the practice under the *Judicature Act*, the rules of pleading are to be regarded as subservient to, and not overriding, truth and justice. As the late Sir Samuel Way used to say, 'the trial judge is not umpiring a game of chance or skill, he is administering justice'...

On the other hand, the current position of the law appears to run counter to the rationale for including Rule 3(1) in Order 16 of the *National Court Rules*. The *raison d'être* and the very essence of the sub-rule appears to be the provision of an exclusive procedure for enforcing the constitutional provisions relating to judicial review. For this reason, it is categorically stated that "*No application for judicial review shall be made unless the leave of the court has been obtained in accordance with this Rule.*"[25] Of course, judges have the discretion to dispense with compliance with the rules of court at any time, whether before or after the

---

circumstances and in view of the apparent defects mentioned, to treat this as an application for judicial review.

[20] [1907] 1 KB 1; [1904-07] All ER 1251.

[21] See *Polling v Motor Vehicles Insurance (PNG) Trust* [1986] PNGLR 228.

[22] See *Novau*, above, note 19.

[23] Above, note 20 at 4 and 1252, respectively.

[24] [1964] SASR 163 at 171.

[25] Order 16 Rule 3 (1) of the *National Court Rules*. (Emphasis added.)

time for compliance arises.[26] Furthermore, unless the court so directs, non-compliance with the rules of court does not render any proceedings void.[27] Hence, the categorical imperative of Rule 3(1) of Order 16 cannot be considered as absolute.

Nevertheless, without disputing the discretion conferred by Order 1 Rules 7 and 8 of the *National Court Rules*, and while acknowledging the overriding importance of justice and the consequent need to make the rules of procedure subservient to it, it may still be necessary to fine-tune the relationship of the rules of procedure to the *Constitution* if the provisions of the *Constitution* are to be enforced in a systematic and ordered manner. Clearly, the power of judicial review is derived from the *Constitution* and not the *National Court Rules*. Hence, the application for judicial review mentioned in Order 16 Rule 3(1) of the *National Court Rules* refers to the constitutional power of judicial review. This means that if the constitutional powers are taken in isolation from the sub-rule and regarded as a separate procedure for bringing an application for judicial review, then the sub-rule would become meaningless and totally unnecessary.

The corollary of this argument is that, granted that rules of court are not legislative and, therefore, do not carry statutory force, still the supplementary role that they play in the enforcement of statutory and constitutional powers cannot and should not be lightly dismissed. Indeed, without the rules of court, the statutory and constitutional powers cannot be systematically enforced. Hence, the fact that the *Constitution* empowers the National Court to make certain orders should not negate the procedure prescribed by Order 16 of the *National Court Rules* for invoking the power.

In *More v University of PNG*,[28] where Pratt J had the opportunity to comment on a similar situation, he stated what may be considered as a highly refined definition of the relationship of the rules of procedure to the *Constitution*. As he aptly put it:

> In civil proceedings it is essential to observe and follow established practice and procedure if for no other reason than to avoid confusion, uncertainty and the consequences which are either unexpected or unsought or both...

[26] Ref. Order 1 Rule 7 of the *National Court Rules*.
[27] Ref. Order 1 Rule 8 of the *National Court Rules*.
[28] [1985] PNGLR 401.

> The relevant practice and procedure of the civil law is applicable to proceedings to enforce the *Constitution*. Any reliance on the *Constitution* should not disregard the Rules of Court.
> The mere fact that one can invoke the *Constitution*, s 57, does not mean that the practice and procedure of the civil law governing the type of application should be disregarded.[29]

This fine-tuning of the relationship of the rules of procedure to the *Constitution*, in my humble opinion, provides a powerful and logical argument for abiding by the restriction imposed by Order 16 Rule 3(1) of the *National Court Rules*. This restriction calls for disallowing a choice of procedures and adopting a single unified procedure for invoking the constitutional power of judicial review. The argument in favour of adopting this position is further strengthened by the fact that, while there are already relatively well-developed and systematic principles in place under the Order 16 procedure for bringing applications for judicial review, there are no comparable established principles or procedure for applications brought under sections 23(3) and 155(4) of the *Constitution*.

---

[29] *Id*., pp. 405, 407.

CHAPTER 4

ORDER 16 PROCEDURE FOR OBTAINING LEAVE

Relevant Forms for Applying for Leave

Order 16 Rule 3 of the *National Court Rules* (Ch 38) lays down the procedure for applying for leave. According to this Rule, an application for leave must be instituted by originating summons *ex parte* to the National Court or to a judge in chambers, if the Court is in vacation.[1] In practice, an application for leave to apply for judicial review is not heard in the normal course of events in open court. On the contrary, in order to expedite the hearing of the application, it proceeds by way of originating summons to a judge in chambers. Characteristically, an application can be expected to be heard within two or three weeks. Urgent cases, however, can be heard, if necessary, within hours rather than weeks.

The *ex parte* application must be supported :

1. by a statement setting out the name and description of the applicant, the relief sought and the grounds on which the relief is sought; and
2. an affidavit, to be filed before the application is made, verifying the facts relied on.[2]

According to the Rule, the minimum relevant forms necessary for filing an application for leave are: the Originating Summons, Statement in Support, Supporting Affidavit, Notice to the Secretary of Justice, and Statement of Claims for Damages, if necessary.

1. Originating Summons

The application for leave to apply for judicial review is made by originating summons *ex parte* to the National Court by filing a notice of application at the National Court Registry. This must indicate the source of the powers of the court, whether inherent, constitutional or statutory,

[1] The appropriate form for filing this application is Form 6.
[2] Order 16 Rule 3(2).

which the applicant seeks to invoke. For example, "The Plaintiff claims :- Leave to proceed with this application for judicial review pursuant to the provisions of Order 16 Rule 3(1) of the *National Court Rules* (Ch 38)". A standard format for the originating summons is prescribed by Form 6 of Schedule 1 to the *National Court Rules* (Ch 38). The use of the standard prescribed form does not prohibit the attachment of additional information separately. Indeed, such an attachment is expressly permitted by Rule 3(2)(a) and will be necessary, particularly, where numerous forms of relief are sought or where numerous grounds are relied upon.

2. Statement in Support

The application for leave must be supported by a Statement in Support of the Originating Summons filed pursuant to the provisions of Order 16 Rule 3(2)(a) of the *National Court Rules* (Ch 38). This must set out the following information:

(a) the name and description of the applicant;
(b) the relief sought and legal evidence to support the grounds upon which it is sought;
(c) the name and address of the applicant's counsel (if any); and
(d) the applicant's address for service.

Since it describes the crux of the applicant's complaint, defines the relevant legal issues and guides the court in its decision-making process, the nature of the relief sought is the most important thing at the time of filing the application. This must, therefore, be clearly specified without resort to unrealistic and hypothetical forms of relief, and must take into account the purpose and function of the judicial review process. Hence, for example, if an application seeks to challenge the exercise of a discretionary power, it is no use asking the court to order that the discretion be exercised in the applicant's favour. The appropriate relief, and one that the court will normally grant, is *certiorari* to quash the purported exercise of the discretion and an order that the discretion be exercised properly. However, in order to take advantage of the courts' inherent power under section 155(4) of the *Constitution* to make any orders that are necessary to do justice in the circumstances of a particular case, as a matter of strategy, it is advisable to always invoke this power. This may be done by requesting the court, as the last relief sought, to make any other orders, pursuant to section 155(4) of the *Constitution*, as it may deem necessary to do justice in the particular circumstances of the case.

It must be borne in mind that, although Order 16 provides that "no grounds shall be relied on or any relief sought at the hearing [of the full application for judicial review] except the grounds and relief set out in the statement",[3] it also provides express power for the Court to "allow the applicant's statement to be amended, whether by specifying different or additional grounds of relief or otherwise, on such terms as it thinks fit."[4] Generally, many judges exercise their discretion under this Rule to permit amendments[5] and renewal of applications. In practice, therefore, an application for leave to apply for judicial review is rarely struck out simply because the statement in support has not fully detailed the relief sought or the grounds relied upon. It may be advisable, however, if an applicant intends to apply to amend the statement in support, to give notice of this intention in advance.

3. Supporting Affidavit

The application for leave must be accompanied by an affidavit verifying the statement filed pursuant to the provisions of Order 16 Rule 3(2)(b) of the *National Court Rules* (Ch 38). The requirement of an affidavit commits an applicant to stating the facts relied upon and the basis of the case on oath. This makes the applicant liable in perjury.

Since this affidavit will form an important basis of the applicant's application for judicial review, if leave is granted, it is crucial that the

---

[3] Rule 6(1).

[4] Rule 3(4). The court is empowered to do the same at the full hearing also and may even allow further affidavits to be used if they deal with new matters arising out of an affidavit of any other party to the application. Rule 6(2).

[5] Judges also have the discretion under Order 1 Rule 7 of the *National Court Rules* to dispense with compliance with the rules at any time, whether before or after the time for compliance arises. Order 1 Rule 8 of the *National Court Rules* provides that non-compliance with any of the rules does not render any proceedings void unless the court so directs.

affidavit must contain all the basic material facts on which reliance will be placed. The stipulated facts must contain the reasons for any delay in making the application in order to satisfy the court that the delay is not undue or prejudicial and that there are "good reasons" under Rule 4 of Order 16 to grant leave.[6]

The fact that the application is made *ex parte* places a positive duty to disclose all material facts in the supporting affidavit in order not to mislead the court. This duty rests primarily on the applicant but also applies to the applicant's counsel, as they owe a duty to the court to be frank in making *ex parte* applications. Counsel must, therefore, satisfy themselves that they are fully aware of the material facts which ought to be disclosed, bearing in mind that a lack of candour at the *ex parte* stage may be taken into account by the court in any later application by the respondent to challenge the grant of leave or at the full hearing where the court decides whether discretionary remedies under Order 16 should be granted.

Pursuant to the provision for discovery in applications for judicial review, if leave is granted, further affidavit evidence dealing with new matters arising out of an affidavit of any other party may be lodged, with the permission of the court, in support of the application for judicial review. The applicant, therefore, has the opportunity, if any of his supporting evidence on oath is challenged by the respondent, to lodge further affidavits in reply. For this reason, it is not necessary nor desirable to overburden the supporting affidavit at the leave stage. This approach has the merit of saving costs as well as preventing the court from being overburdened with unnecessary, unchallenged factual material.

4. Notice to the Secretary of Justice

Order 16 Rule 3(3) of the *National Court Rules* (Ch 38) requires that,

---

[6] Many late applications fail not because of the delay in instituting the action, but simply because of the absence of any explanation for the delay. See *Kaupa v Register of Workers Compensation* (1995) N 1300 and *Application of Evangelical Lutheran Church of PNG* [1995] PNGLR 267; (1995) N1317.

> application is made and must at the same time lodge with the Secretary copies of the statement and every affidavit in support.

According to this Rule, it is mandatory to give at least two days' notice to the Secretary for Justice before the application is made. This notice is effected by delivery of a sealed copy of the originating summons with the return date for the hearing of the application for leave duly endorsed thereon. At the same time as notice is given, the Secretary must also be served with copies of the statement and every affidavit in support of the application, including the affidavit verifying. This documentation need not be served personally on the Secretary for Justice. The service may be effected by leaving the documents at the Secretary's office in the Department of Justice with the person apparently occupying the position of the personal secretary to the Secretary.[7]

The rationale for requiring notice to be given to the Secretary for Justice is to enable the State to appear on the preliminary application and, if necessary, to oppose the grant of leave if the application relates to a matter of public interest or public policy.[8]

5. Statement of Claim for Damages

An applicant for leave may, if he has a claim for damages arising from any matter to which the application relates, also incorporate such a claim in the statement in support of his application.[9] This is optional, depending upon the circumstances. However, if such a claim is made, it must be made pursuant to the provisions of Order 16 Rule 2 of the *National Court Rules* (Ch 38).

The express power of the Court under Order 16 Rule 3(4) of the *National Court Rules* (Ch 38) to allow amendment and, indeed, the general power of the National Court under Order 1 Rule 7 of the *National Court Rules* to dispense with compliance with the rules at any time, whether before or after the time for compliance arises, apply equally to claims for damages in judicial review applications. This is so

---

[7] Order 16 Rule 12.

[8] Ref. *NTN v PTC* [1987] PNGLR 70, pp. 73-74.

[9] Order 16 Rule 7(1).

notwithstanding Order 16 Rule 7, which provides that the Court may only award damages in an application for judicial review where they have been included in the statement in support of the application for leave. In practice, however, in order not to undermine the protection afforded by Order 16 Rule 7, and because the normal rules of pleading apply to claims for damages under Order 16, the Court is unlikely to permit such amendments unless they are made in good time and with adequate notice. It is, therefore, advisable to include any claim for damages in the statement at the time of filing the application.

CHAPTER 5
EX PARTE APPLICATION

Controversy About *Ex Parte* Procedure

There is general agreement that if the issues raised in an application for leave are of no concern to the State and, for that reason, the Secretary for Justice makes no appearance or gives no indication to participate, then the application for leave is required to proceed *ex parte* without notice to any interested or potentially interested party. However, there is a raging controversy about the meaning of the phrase "*ex parte*". The question is whether or not intervention by other parties may be permitted in an *ex parte* proceeding. Even if it is not, does the Court have the discretion to direct interested or potentially interested parties to intervene? If so, under what circumstances may it exercise this discretion? And, if intervention is permitted, may the Court hear arguments relating to the substantive matter of the case at this stage of the application for judicial review?

Supreme Court Ruling on the Meaning of *Ex Parte*

Before the Order 16 procedure came into effect, the Supreme Court had twice indicated that a hearing "*ex parte*" means, strictly, a hearing without notice to the party affected; that is, a hearing in the absence of the defendant.[1] In *Ombudsman Commission v Donohoe*,[2] when the Supreme Court had the occasion to interpret the phrase as it applies in the context of Order 16, Amet J (as he then was) stated that:

> ... an application for leave to file an application for judicial review ... is *ex parte* and so the Court does not have any other material contesting the application. I consider that the substantial issues raised are matters properly to be considered by the court hearing the

---

[1] Ref. *R. v Mitchell; Ex parte Wafing* [1973] PNGLR 461 and *Peter v South Pacific Brewery Ltd* [1976] PNGLR 537.

[2] [1985] PNGLR 348.

> substantive application, depending on its conclusion of facts upon an assessment of all the evidence and the benefit of legal arguments.[3]

This *dicta* implies that intervention by other parties is not only precluded at the preliminary stage of applying for leave but also that the courts are not required at this stage to hear arguments relating to the substantive matter of the case. Another logical inference that may be made from the *dicta* is that the merits or demerits of the substantive legal issues of an application for leave to apply for judicial review have no bearing whatsoever on the decision to grant or refuse leave.

Deviations from the Supreme Court Ruling

Notwithstanding the precedent established by the Supreme Court on this issue, McDermott AJ took a strangely divergent position in *Olasco Niugini Pty Ltd v Kaputin.*[4] The applicant in this case sought leave to apply for judicial review of the decision of the Minister for Petroleum and Energy which purported to grant a petroleum prospecting licence to Kelvin Energy Ltd., the seventh respondent. Without any reference to the binding decision of the Supreme Court on the issue, His Honour held that leave should be granted to each of the seven respondents, including the State, to intervene and be heard in the application for leave to apply for judicial review.

Intervention by the State is, of course, expressly permitted under Order 16 of the *National Court Rules* (Ch 38). However, in the absence of any express permission to allow intervention by the respondents to an application for leave, the Court's order granting leave to the other six respondents to intervene certainly raised questions about the procedural propriety of the order. Without distinguishing the position of the State from that of the other respondents, His Honour conceded that intervention (presumably by the six respondents) was not expressly provided for in Order 16. He, however, contended that the provisions of Order 16 Rule 3, particularly the clause "must be made by originating summons ex parte to the Court", do not preclude intervention by other

---

[3] *Id.*, at 361. This decision has been affirmed by the Supreme Court in the case of *Geno v PNG* [1993] PNGLR 22.

[4] [1986] PNGLR 244.

parties at the leave stage of the judicial review process. According to him,

> The necessity for leave was well explained in *Inland Revenue Commissioners; Ex parte National Federation of Self-Employed and Small Businesses Ltd* [1981] 2 WLR 722 where Lord Diplock said at p 739:
>
> > 'Its purpose is to prevent the time of the court being wasted by busybodies with misguided and trivial complaints of administrative errors, and to remove the uncertainty in which public officers and authorities might be left as to whether they could safely proceed with administrative action while proceedings for judicial review of it were actually pending even though misconceived.'
>
> As Lord Scarman said at p 749:
>
> > 'The curb represented by the need for an applicant to show, when he seeks leave to apply, that he has an interest in such a case is an essential protection against abuse of legal process. It enables the court to prevent abuse by busybodies, cranks, and other mischief-makers.'
>
> It appears to me implicit in this reasoning that a court may hear argument at the preliminary stage, although not expressly mentioned in the rules relating to the grant of leave to apply (as distinct from the hearing of the application...[5]

The reliance on these *dicta* to support intervention by the respondents to an application for leave to apply for judicial review, on close analysis, reveals some confusion. This is because, apart from the fact there is no reference whatsoever to the phrase "*ex parte*" in the *dicta,* it is patently clear from the context of Lord Diplock's statement that the subject matter of his discussion was the rationale for requiring an applicant to obtain leave before invoking the judicial review jurisdiction of the courts.[6] Similarly, Lord Scarman's statement was made in the context of justifying the requirement of sufficient interest before an applicant is granted leave.[7] These statements, quoted out of context, clearly provide no support for permitting intervention by the respondents nor for hearing

---

[5] *Id.*, p. 245.

[6] As a preface to his statement, Lord Diplock said, "The need for leave to start proceedings for remedies in public law is not new". *Inland Revenue Commissioners v National Federation of Self-Employed and Small Businesses Ltd* [1981] 2 WLR 722 at 739, also [1982] AC 617 at 642 and [1981] 2 All ER 93 at 105.

[7] The sub-heading under which Lord Scarman's statement appeared was specifically titled "The Interest". *Id.*, pp. 748, 653 and 113, respectively.

arguments relating to the substantive issues during the *ex parte* proceedings of an application for leave.

Perhaps the more relevant *dicta* that could possibly have provided some support for McDermott AJ's decision, instead of those quoted, is Lord Diplock's statement made in the same case that:

> The procedure under the new Ord 53 involves two stages: (1) the application for leave to apply for judicial review, and (2) if leave is granted, the hearing of the application itself. The former, or 'threshold', stage is regulated by r 3. The application for leave to apply for judicial review is made initially ex parte, *but may be adjourned for the persons or bodies against whom relief is sought to be represented.*[8]

This statement, though not supported by any express provisions of Order 53 of the *Rules of the Supreme Court* (U.K.), which is the English version of Order 16 of the *National Court Rules* (Ch 38), carries considerable weight, coming from the one of the greatest English authorities on judicial review. Another possible support for McDermott AJ's decision is Lord Fraser of Tullybelton's concurring judgment in the same case, which implied that intervention by the respondent may be permitted. In that judgment, the English Lord stated that:

> *I recognise that in some cases, perhaps in many, it may be impracticable to decide whether an applicant has a sufficient interest or not, without having evidence from both parties as to the matter to which the application relates*, and that, in such cases, the court before whom the matter comes in the first instance cannot refuse leave to the applicant at the *ex parte* stage, under rule 3(5). The court which grants leave at that stage will do so on the footing that it makes a provisional finding of sufficient interest, subject to revisal later on, and it is therefore not necessarily to be criticised merely because the final decision is that the applicant did not have sufficient interest. *But where, after seeing the evidence of both parties*, the proper conclusion is that the applicant did not have a sufficient interest to make the application, the decision ought to be made on that ground.[9]

The logical inference from these two statements is that the English courts may permit intervention by the respondent to submit evidence and be heard during an application for leave to apply for judicial review. If that is so, then the statements do provide some authority for McDermott AJ's decision. Unfortunately, however, apart from the fact that post-

[8] *Id.*, at pp. 738, 642 and 105, respectively. (Emphasis added.)

[9] *Id.*, at pp. 741, 645 and 107, respectively. (Emphasis added.)

independence English authorities are not binding in Papua New Guinea, the English practice in this area of the law is in clear conflict with the Supreme Court ruling on the issue. For this reason, even if the above statements of the English Lords had been cited in the Olasco Niugini case, they could not have rendered the decision any more valid.

McDermott AJ's back-up argument in support of allowing intervention by the respondents was that:

> Because of the urgency involved I see no reason why the application for leave and the hearing of the application for judicial review could not proceed simultaneously as is often the case in appeals...[10]

This argument, taken literally, seems to suggest that, if the urgency of the situation warrants it, then notwithstanding the *ex parte* nature of the proceedings, the Court has a discretion to hear arguments relating to the substantive matter during the preliminary stage of applying for leave.

In the first place, this argument is not supported by any authority, and His Honour did not provide any himself. Secondly, on the face of it, the argument clearly runs counter to the provisions of Order 16 of the *National Court Rules* (Ch 38)[11] and the Supreme Court ruling on the issue. Furthermore, the comparison between judicial review proceedings and an appeal also seems to have overlooked the fundamental differences between the two proceedings. The distinction between these two proceedings, which is now well established in law, is the crucial point that even in cases where no appeal lies against an order or a decision, judicial review would, nevertheless, still be available to challenge the validity or reasonableness of the order or decision.[12] For this reason, the law deliberately establishes a different procedure for invoking the judicial review process than for instituting an appeal. The urgency of the situation of a case, therefore, is no basis for substituting an appeal procedure for the procedure prescribed by law for applying for judicial review and cannot, therefore, be used to justify intervention at the leave stage.

---

[10] Above, note 4 at 247.

[11] Order 16 specifies two distinct stages for applying for judicial review: the first is the application for leave to apply for judicial review (regulated by Rule 3) and the second is the application for judicial review (governed by Rule 5).

[12] Ref. *Ombudsman Commission*, above, note 2.

Although open to criticism on the grounds of non-compliance with the procedure prescribed under Order 16 and inconsistency with the Supreme Court decision on the meaning of *ex parte* proceedings, McDermott AJ's decision is not altogether without merit. It will be recalled that His Honour acknowledged the relevant provisions of Order 16 and openly admitted that his decision to grant leave to the defendants to intervene and be heard in the application for leave to apply for judicial review deviated from the express provisions of Order 16. Furthermore, on account of the deviation, His Honour attempted to justify his decision on different grounds. Thus, even though the attempt is not wholly successful, the mere expression of the awareness of a possible conflict and the consequent attempt to provide a justification for deviating is a commendable approach to judicial decision-making. This approach contrasts sharply with that adopted by Wilson J in *NTN Pty Ltd v PTC*.[13]

In that case, the applicant sought leave to apply for judicial review of the decision of the Board of the Post and Telecommunication Corporation (PTC) which granted broadcasting licences to Media Niugini (the third defendant). Wilson J granted leave to the Board of PTC and PTC (the first and second defendants, respectively) and Media Niugini to intervene and to make submissions. Incidentally, this decision was made over the formal objection of the applicant. Although the decision to allow such intervention was clearly contrary to Rule 3(2) of Order 16, His Honour granted the leave as a matter of course, without adverting his mind to the Rule. Delivering his judgment, His Honour stated that:

> 1. The application before me on 16 April was an *ex parte* application with only the legal representatives of NTN in court.
> 2. On 22 April 1987 when the matter resumed for me to deliver judgment Mr Hirst, counsel for Media Niugini, successfully sought leave to appear to present submissions on behalf of his client regarding the element of delay in applying for relief which was a matter going to the exercise of my discretion as to whether leave should be granted to NTN. The application for leave was contested by Mr. Glenn on behalf of NTN. After giving the matter consideration I gave a ruling in the following terms:
>
> 'I have before me an application by Media Niugini (MNG) for leave to appear and make representations in relation to an

[13] [1987] PNGLR 70.

> application for leave for judicial review by NTN Pty Ltd (NTN). That application revolves around matters covered by O 16, r 4 which deals with the situation where the court's discretion is being exercised where there is delay.
>
> I take the view that this provision is in the Rules to give some protection to the rights of parties affected as in this case MNG clearly will be. During the initial hearing I indicated my concern that I was unable to come to any view on what I termed the 'second leg' of O 16, r 4, because I had nothing before me on which to base my decision as to the discretion given.
>
> The application now before me would enable such information to be to hand. I have no doubt that MNG has sufficient interest to seek leave and I consider it would be fair to allow such a course...
>
> The applicant, MNG, should be given leave for the purpose of presenting its case in relation to those matters requiring this Court's attention made under O 16, r 4, and I so order.'
>
> 3. On 29 April 1987 the case resumed after further affidavit evidence had been filed by Media Niugini and by NTN in reply.
>
> Mr. Steele, counsel appearing on behalf of PTC, sought leave to make submissions on behalf of his client and such leave was granted over the formal objection of NTN.
>
> Mr G Thorley the Chief Executive Officer of Media Niugini was also examined on his two affidavits.
>
> Submissions were then heard relating to the issue of delay.[14]

From the account of these events, it is not clear on what grounds NTN objected to the grant of leave to the respondents to intervene and to make submissions. However, the reasons adduced by His Honour for granting leave for intervention do not seem to address the pertinent issues involved here. In the first place, since the course of action taken by His Honour was in clear conflict with Rule 3(2) of Order 16, which requires applications for leave to apply for judicial review to be heard *ex parte*, as a matter of principle, it would have been most pertinent to address this issue and then justify deviation from the Order 16 procedure.

Secondly, while conceding the difficulty that judges may face in making a decision on the issue of delay if the evidence available to the

[14] *Id.*, pp. 71-72.

Court does not adequately address the issue,[15] that still does not justify deviation from the rules of procedure. The problem of insufficient evidence at the leave stage of the judicial review proceedings is one that can hardly be avoided because of the summary nature of the proceedings. However, as Hinchliffe J rightly points out, the statement and the affidavit verifying the facts "are adequate for the Judge to decide whether or not to grant leave."[16] Wilson J holds a similar view. As he explained, the provisions of Order 16 Rule 4 require the court, in determining undue delay, to take into account two separate matters. The first is the time limit stated in the Rule and the other is whether granting the relief sought "would be likely to cause substantial hardship to, or substantially prejudice the rights of, any person or would be detrimental to good administration". According to him, in considering these matters, the courts have traditionally relied upon, and found sufficient information from, the originating summons and the statement in support to make a decision.[17]

It is important to bear in mind, as Lord Diplock emphasises, that the leave application, aside from being an *ex parte* proceeding, is a "threshold" stage of the judicial review process,

> ... in the sense that the court is only required to form a *prima facie* view about the case based upon the material that is available at the first stage. The *prima facie* view so formed, if favourable to the applicant, may alter on further consideration in the light of further evidence that may be before the court at the second stage, the hearing of the application for judicial review itself.[18]

It is, therefore, not absolutely necessary nor required at the leave stage to have substantial evidence or to receive submissions from the respondent and hear arguments on the issue before a decision on leave is made. Indeed, a prolonged hearing of the leave application, as exemplified by this case, clearly detracts from the summary nature of the process and runs counter to the objectives of Order 16.

---

[15] It would seem that this was one of the reasons, though not fully spelt out, why Mc Dermott AJ granted leave to the respondents in *Olasco Niugini Pty Ltd v Kaputin* to intervene and be heard in an application for leave for judicial review.

[16] *Manjin v PTC* [1990] PNGLR 288 at 289.

[17] See *Ex parte Gurupa* (1990) N856; *Re Nagi Clan* [1995] PNGLR 13; (1991) N1036.

[18] *Inland Revenue Commissioners; Ex parte National Federation of Self-Employed and Small Businesses Ltd* [1981] 2 WLR 722 at 738; [1982] AC 617 at 642; [1981] 2 All ER 93 at 105.

Finally, even if His Honour's argument that the objective of Order 16 Rule 4 is to give some protection to the rights of other parties that may be affected by an application for leave to apply for judicial review were conceded, it still would not justify intervention by other parties in the *ex parte* proceedings. This is because the provisions of Order 16 Rule 3(5) clearly make the sufficient interest of the applicant the basis for granting or refusing an application for leave to apply for judicial review, and not the interest of the respondent to the application. To suggest, as His Honour does, that because the respondent has a sufficient interest to seek leave, it would, therefore, be fair to allow intervention confuses the issue of sufficient interest and has no legal support whatsoever.

The issue arose again in *Diro v Ombudsman Commission.*[19] In this case, the plaintiff applied for leave to challenge the validity of the Ombudsman Commission's referrals of findings to the Public Prosecutor. Presumably, because the defendant had been served with notice of the application, counsel for the defendant sought leave, on the authority of the decision of McDermott AJ in *Olasco Niugini Pty Ltd v Kaputin*[20] and Wilson J in *NTN Pty Ltd v PTC,*[21] to intervene and to file an affidavit to support submissions in opposition. Sheehan J rejected the two authorities but, nevertheless, granted leave to the defendant to intervene in the application for leave to apply for judicial review. The intervention was permitted, ostensibly because "because the Court wished to hear argument on the relevant law and on the substance of the grounds set out in this application and because, in any case, the plaintiff did not oppose intervention".[22]

Conscious of the possible contradiction in rejecting the authorities cited and yet allowing intervention in the *ex parte* proceedings, His Honour went to great length to distinguish his decision from the authorities and to provide a justification for his judgment. According to him, the authority of the Olasco Niugini case was rejected because "[a]lthough leave to intervene was granted in that case, the arguments in opposition supported by affidavits were heard at the substantive hearing

---

[19] [1991] PNGLR 153.
[20] Above, note 4.
[21] [1987] PNGLR 70.
[22] Above, note 19 at 154.

of the review".[23] The NTN case, on the other hand, was dismissed on the basis that, "leave to intervene and argue against leave was granted to a defendant on issues of undue delay and hardship and affidavits filed in opposition on those grounds were read at the application for leave".[24]

In the instant case, however, the decision only grants leave to intervene and make submissions; it does not grant leave to file and read a supporting affidavit. This approach, according to Sheehan J, cannot be considered as contravening the *ex parte* requirement of Order 16.[25] For, in his view, it is a "better course" to take because it ensures that an application for leave to apply for judicial review remains the *ex parte* application required by Order 16 Rule 3(2). As he expressed it,

> If affidavits are necessary to support an opposition, that contest signals that an argument on the merits is required. That takes the matter beyond the ex parte consideration of whether the applicant has an arguable case on the papers filed, as envisaged by Order 16. It becomes a hearing of the review itself. This does not prevent effective opposition to any application for leave, particularly on grounds of insufficient interest, delay or substantial hardship to a defending party. It does restrict argument to the preliminary ex parte examination intended by the rules.[26]

The validity of these arguments is open to question. In the first place, Sheehan J's view that a restricted argument in opposition to an application for leave is permitted in an *ex parte* application is novel, as it is unfounded. The meaning of an *ex parte* proceeding has been clearly stated by Amet J (as he then was) and Hinchliffe J in *Ombudsman Commission v Donohoe*[27] and in *Manjin v PTC*,[28] respectively. These two cases correctly interpret the requirements of an *ex parte* proceeding as

---

[23] *Ibid.*

[24] *Ibid.*

[25] In *Amadio Pty Ltd v PNG* [1992] PNGLR 218, Woods J, without reference to this case, also used a similar argument to justify granting permission to the defendants to intervene and make submissions. According to him, at p. 220, "[a]ny fair and reasonable consideration of the above [constitutional] provisions must mean that, without forgoing the ex parte principle in urgent applications for leave, any person named in any proceedings and who has a real interest in the matter sought to be reviewed must have a right to be in attendance and to be represented at any hearing which could affect his or her position or rights, subject to the court limiting such appearance to make submissions only on those limited areas where the court feels it needs assistance."

[26] Above, note 19 at 154.

[27] Above, note 2.

[28] Above, note 16.

envisaged by Order 16. According to them, an *ex parte* application means that the court does not have any other material contesting the application and, furthermore, there is no provision or reason for allowing intervention by any other parties. The argument that, provided a supporting affidavit is not filed and read, leave may be granted to the respondent of an application for leave to intervene and make submissions in an *ex parte* proceeding without violating the *ex parte* requirements of Order 16 is, therefore, one that is difficult to substantiate.

Secondly, if intervention by the respondent of an application for leave is not permitted in an *ex parte* application, then it follows that the decision to grant leave cannot be justified by the reason that the applicant does not oppose the intervention. Indeed, one may add that the discretion to grant or refuse leave is one that lies with the court or judge and not the applicant. Unless the Court or judge abdicates its discretion, duty and responsibility to determine the issue of whether to grant or refuse leave, the applicant's view on the issue cannot be substituted for that of the court.

Finally, it appears that His Honour's insistence on the fact that his decision to allow intervention by the defendant was consistent with the *ex parte* requirement of Order 16 was based upon a mistaken belief that there is a requirement under Order 16 for notice to be given to the Ombudsman Commission.[29] This mistaken impression is evident from the passage in which he stated that:

> By the National Court Rules, O 16 r 3(2), application for leave to move for judicial review shall be made ex parte. *Even though there is a requirement for notice to be given to the defendant* there is no automatic right given a defendant to oppose at this stage. But the intervention of the defendant or other parties is not thereby wholly excluded. Others may intervene and oppose ...[30]

The view that the defendant in this case is required to be served notice of the application for leave to apply for judicial review is clearly erroneous. For, under Order 16 Rule 3(2), only the Secretary for Justice, as the representative of the State's interest, is required to be served. The Ombudsman Commission is an independent constitutional body and,

---

[29] See also *Balakau v Ombudsman Commission* [1995] PNGLR 70; (1995) N1397 where the Ombudsman Commission was permitted to intervene in an application for leave in order to argue that leave should not be granted on the ground of delay.

[30] Above, note 19 at 154. (Emphasis added.)

therefore, cannot, for purposes of Order 16, be considered as, nor equated with, the State.

Reform Proposals

Leaving aside all the criticisms that may be levelled against the decisions that deviate from the Supreme Court ruling on the issue, the clearest authority supporting the argument that those decisions are procedurally inaccurate is to be found in *Manjin v PTC*.[31] In this case, counsel for the defendant attempted to use the decision in *Olasco Niugini Pty Ltd v Kaputin* as support for his submission that he should be allowed to intervene in an application for leave to apply for judicial review. Hinchliffe J, however, promptly rejected the submission and pointed out that the service of notice on the defendant had been done in error. In handing down his decision, His Honour laid down the clearest formulation of the law to date on the issue of intervention in *ex parte* proceedings. In a decision which has been affirmed by the Supreme Court, he stated categorically that,

> There is no provision for [the intervention of other parties] under the rules and it would be senseless if there was such a rule because it would not then be an *ex parte* application. An ex parte application, according to *Jowitt's Dictionary of English Law*, (2nd ed, 1977) at 733, 'means that an application is made by one party to a proceeding in the absence of the other.'
> *Webster's New International Dictionary of the English Language*, (2nd ed) at 896 reads 'ex parte - of legal proceedings, ex parte ordinarily implies a hearing or examination in the presence of, or on papers filed by, one party and in the absence of, and often without notice to, the other ...'
> To my mind O16, r 3(2) is clear. There is no need to read anything into it. The application for leave to apply is an ex parte application and there is no provision or reason for allowing intervention by any other parties.[32]

[31] Above, note 16.

[32] *Id.*, p. 290.

These clearly expressed and quite unequivocal principles, it may be observed, are in complete conformity with Order 16 and the Supreme Court ruling on the issue. Yet, surprisingly, they seem to have had little or no impact on the controversy surrounding the issue of intervention in *ex parte* proceedings.

Given the preponderance of cases that have departed from the strict requirements of Order 16 Rule 3(2) regarding *ex parte* proceedings and continue to do so in spite of a Supreme Court ruling on the issue, the question of the validity of the decisions which do not conform with Order 16 or the Supreme Court position becomes a non-issue. In the light of this situation, the only viable option may be a possible legitimization of the deviant procedure. That is to say that judges should be given the discretion to depart from the strict requirements of an *ex parte* proceeding in particular cases if, in their opinion, such a course of action is warranted and necessary to achieve justice. This could be done by amending Order 16 Rule 3(2) of the *National Courts Rules* (Ch 38). The amendment should clearly specify that judges have the discretion to direct interested or potentially interested parties to intervene and make submissions; and to allow the intervening parties to file and read a supporting affidavit; but not to hear arguments relating to the substantive matter of the case at the leave stage of the application for judicial review. Apart from legalizing the deviant procedure, such an amendment would finally lay the controversy surrounding the meaning of the phrase "*ex parte*" to rest. Alternatively, if the Rule is to remain, then it might be necessary to launch a sustained campaign to educate judges about the procedural requirements of the Rule in order to prevent deviations in the future.

PART III

MATTERS RELEVANT TO THE COURT'S DISCRETION

CHAPTER 6

DISCRETION OF THE COURT

Nature of the Court's Discretion

The National Court's discretionary power to grant or refuse relief arises at two different stages in the Order 16 procedure. First, at the initial stage of application for leave, the Court must exercise a discretion as to whether or not to grant leave to apply for judicial review. Second, at the full hearing, the Court may exercise a discretion to grant or refuse any or all of the particular remedies applied for. At both stages, the broad principles relating to the conduct of the applicant, the availability of alternative remedies and the effect of the remedy sought are similar. In all cases, the Court's discretion must be exercised judicially, in the sense that precedent must be followed. However, since the leave to apply stage is concerned only with filtering out applications which are clearly without merit, there are specific legal principles which are particular to this stage alone. The discussion here focuses on these principles.

It should be emphasised that the essence of discretionary power is a flexible response to the circumstances of the individual case. Thus, it should be understood that the legal principles discussed here and in the subsequent chapters provide a guideline or framework for the exercise of the court's discretion. They are not concerned with the factors which the Court is free to take into account in generally balancing the relevant factors in the circumstances of a particular case. This means that while the application of the legal principles may be constant and uniform, in terms of flexibility, the factors that are taken into account in the application of the principles may vary according to the circumstances of the particular case.

Court's Discretion Under Order 16

The first case and the leading authority on the issue of matters relevant to the exercise of the Court's discretion in an application for leave is *Ombudsman Commission v Donohoe*.[1] In that case, the Supreme Court held that:

> On an application for leave to file an application for judicial review, the Court need only be satisfied as to the requirements of O 16, rr 2, 3 and 5... [*sic*] The Court is not required to address the matters specified in O 16, r 1(2). [Per Amet J, as he then was.][2]

In *Valentine v Somare*,[3] Andrew J cited this statement to guide the Court in considering an application for leave. His Honour, however, did not elaborate on the statement and, from his decision, it is not clear how much guide, if any, was derived from it. We shall, therefore, examine the statement briefly in order to find out the extent to which it provides any guide on the issue.

Rule 1(2) of Order 16 deals with cases which are appropriate for application for judicial review. The relevant provisions state as follows:

> 1. (2) An application for a declaration or an injunction may be made by way of an application for judicial review, and on such an application the Court may grant the declaration or injunction claimed if it considers that, having regard to - -
> (a) the nature of the matters in respect of which relief may be granted by way of an order of *mandamus*, prohibition or *certiorari*;
> (b) the nature of the persons and bodies against whom relief may be granted by way of such an order; and
> (c) all the circumstances of the case,
> it would be just and convenient for the declaration or injunction to be granted on the application for judicial review.

This sub-rule makes relief by way of declaration or injunction a form of judicial review and gives the Court jurisdiction to grant such relief whenever, in its discretion, it is appropriate to do so, having regard to the factors mentioned. In view of the fact that the *Constitution* bestows unlimited jurisdiction on the National Court,[4] and also gives it an

---

[1] [1985] PNGLR 348.
[2] *Id.*, p. 361.
[3] [1988-89] PNGLR 51.
[4] Ref. section 166 of the *Constitution*.

inherent power to review any exercise of judicial authority,[5] and to make orders in the nature of prerogative writs and such orders as are necessary to do justice in the circumstances of a particular case,[6] the jurisdiction conferred by Rule 1(2) may be considered superfluous and, therefore, not required to be addressed. Besides, on a strict interpretation of Order 16, these are not matters to be taken into account in granting or refusing leave. Amet J's interpretation of the rule can, therefore, not be faulted.[7]

Coming to the Supreme Court's ruling on the requirements that need to satisfied in an application for leave, there are a couple of overstatements that need to be pointed out. Before doing that, we must first note that, although not expressly stated, it is reasonable to assume that the provisions of Order 16 referred to in Amet J's statement regarding the requirements that need to satisfied refer to sub-rules 2, 3, and 5 of Rule 3. The *dicta*, however, omits the reference to Rule 3.

Order 16 Rule 3 provides as follows:

> 3. Grant of leave to apply for judicial review (UK 53/3)
>
> (2) An application for leave must be made by originating summons *ex parte* to the Court, except in vacation when it may be made to a Judge in chambers, and must be supported --
>
> (a) by a statement setting out the name and description of the applicant, the relief sought and the grounds on which it is sought; and
>
> (b) by affidavit, to be filed before the application is made, verifying the facts relied on.
>
> (3) The applicant must give notice of the application to the Secretary for Justice not later than two days before the application is made and must at the same time lodge with the Secretary copies of the statement and every affidavit in support.
>
> ...
>
> (5) The Court shall not grant leave unless it considers that the applicant has a sufficient interest in the matter to which the application relates.

---

[5] Ref. section 155(3) of the *Constitution*.

[6] Ref. section 155(4) of the *Constitution*.

[7] Cf., however, the approach of those cases in which the criterion of an arguable case is determined by the actual arguability of a case. It appears from that approach that the factors listed in Rule 1(2), upon which the discretion to grant the reliefs listed may be based, have sometimes been taken into consideration in determining an application for leave.

All these provisions deal with the mode of applying for leave. Hence, while Amet J is obviously correct in regarding sub-rule 5 (the requirement of sufficient interest) as a relevant matter for the exercise of the Court's discretion on leave, the same cannot be said with regard to sub-rules 2 and 3. Admittedly, since Rule 3 of Order 16 deals with the "Grant of leave to apply for judicial review", it may not be incorrect to regard the matters stipulated in these sub-rules as matters relevant to the exercise of discretion in an application for leave. However, if that be the case then, by logical extension, all the other five sub-rules of Rule 3 could also be so regarded. This, of course, would result in an absurdity and could not have been intended by the framers of the *National Court Rules*. In order to avoid such an absurdity, it is important to distinguish the directions to applicants for leave and those to the Court.

Sub-rules 2 and 3 specify the procedure for applying for leave. From the wording and purpose of these sub-rules, there is a clear indication that these are supposed to be instructions to applicants on how to file an application for leave. Sub-rule 5, on the other hand, is definitely a direction to the Court on what it should take into account in considering whether to grant leave or not.

Of course, it could be argued that since the statement regarding the requirements that need to satisfied was made within the context of explaining the implications of an *ex parte* application, it may not be entirely out of place to regard sub-rules 2 and 3 as relevant matters for the court's exercise of discretion. While this argument may justify the consideration of the sub-rule in a particular case, it cannot support the position that the sub-rule is required to be considered in every application for leave. Being an instruction to applicants on how to file an application for leave, once the applicant follows the procedure prescribed in the sub-rules, that is the end of their relevance. In any case, even if an applicant does not fully comply with the procedure laid down in the sub-rules, that does not have a direct impact on the decision on leave. Under sub-rule 4 of Rule 3, the Court is empowered, upon an application for amendment by the applicant, to allow the applicant's statement to be amended and resubmitted. Hence, sub-rules 2 and 3 do not become issues and, therefore, cannot for any other reason be considered as matters relevant to the exercise of the Court's discretion pertaining to the decision on leave.

Apart from the overstatements regarding sub-rules 2 and 3 of Rule 3, there are fundamental omissions in Amet J's statement that need to be addressed. In the first place, the statement omits a second principle, the principle of delay, which is prescribed by Order 16 as a relevant matter for the exercise of the Court's discretion. Rule 4(1) of Order 16 directs the Court, if it thinks that there has been undue delay in making an application, to refuse leave. The consideration of this principle as a relevant matter in the exercise of the Court's discretion in applications for leave, as demonstrated later, is amply supported by judicial practice. Accordingly, even if we consider Amet J's statement as limited to only an interpretation of Order 16 concerning the matters that the Court is required to take into account in the decision on leave, it falls short of comprehensively stating the relevant matters specified by Order 16.

Viewed from the wider context of all the relevant criteria for making a decision on leave, Amet J's statement appears to be even more incomplete. As illustrated in the diagram below, in addition to the two principles (i.e. *locus standi* and delay) specified in Order 16, there are two other legal principles which are also regarded as relevant matters that the Court is required to take into consideration in deciding on leave. These are the requirements that the applicant must have an arguable case and must have exhausted all the available administrative remedies. Any statement regarding the relevant matters to be considered by the Court in an application for leave, therefore, cannot be complete without mention of these two additional criteria. Thus, while Amet J's statement provides a lead on the matters relevant to the exercise of the Court's discretion, in order to be complete, the statement has to be supplemented by reference to the three other criteria that are omitted in the statement.

Relevant Matters for the Court's Discretion

The relevant matters for the exercise of the Court's discretion in determining an application for leave to apply for judicial review may, therefore, be classified under four legal principles. These are *locus standi*, undue delay, an arguable case, and exhaustion of administrative remedies. (See diagram below on the graphic illustration of the principles.)

RELEVANT LEGAL PRINCIPLES FOR A DECISION ON LEAVE

SUFFICIENT INTEREST		ARGUABLE CASE	EXHAUSTION	UNDUE DELAY	
INTEREST	SUFFICIENT	LEGAL ISSUE	ADMINISTRATIVE REMEDIES	CERTIORARI	OTHER REMEDIES
Any interest	Any link or relationship between the applicant and the subject matter of the application.	Fundamental or substantial, genuine or serious legal issue (e.g. constitutional or statutory interpretation to ascertain legislative intent) and not mrerely a factual issue (e.g. scientific or technical matters requiring a factual determination.	Administrative remedies available per statutory appeal procedures must be exhausted such that the decision being challenged is the final rule or order of the highest administrative body or official within the hierarchy of authorities.	Time limit for instituting action is 4 months after the date of the decision that is being challenged.	Action must be brought within a reasonable time.
Social, economic, political, legal, equitable, commercial, etc.				No substantial hardship or substantial prejudice to the rights of any person or detrimental effect on good administration if relief sought is granted.	

The first two principles are specifically laid down by Order 16 of the *National Court Rules* (Ch 38). The other two, adopted from the English common law, have become part of the underlying law of Papua New Guinea and are, therefore, also considered as relevant matters for the exercise of the Court's discretion in granting or refusing leave. These four legal principles are examined in following chapters in the order listed above.

CHAPTER 7

LOCUS STANDI

The test for determining the *locus standi* of an applicant for judicial review is expressed by Order 16 Rule 3(5) of the *National Court Rules* (Ch 38) in the following words of limitation:

> The Court shall not grant leave unless it considers that the applicant has a sufficient interest in the matter to which the application relates.

The task of the courts, therefore, is to determine what constitutes "sufficient interest". Unfortunately, since the *National Court Rules* (Ch 38) do not define the term, presumably leaving it to the discretion of the courts to determine its meaning and content, the Rules provide no guide on how to deal with the task. In the exercise of their discretion, the courts in Papua New Guinea have consistently relied upon the English common law rules as a guide to understanding the meaning and application of the term "sufficient interest". In order to gain a clear understanding of the law in Papua New Guinea, therefore, it is pertinent to review the relevant English common law rules pertaining to the term.

Common Law Rules and Principles

An examination of the English common law rules shows that the term "sufficient interest" incorporates the common law requirement that any person who seeks to invoke the judicial review jurisdiction of the courts must first have standing, or *locus standi*. The principles of this requirement are embodied in the doctrine of *locus standi* which, according to Stein:

> ... denote the existence of a right of an individual or group of individuals (not necessarily constituting a legal entity) to have a court enter upon an adjudication of an issue brought before that court by proceedings instigated by the individual or group. That right once founded, exists apart from the factual or legal merits of the issue brought before the court or the jurisdiction of the court to adjudicate upon the issue. Although the very existence of courts as an institutional mechanism for dispute settlement might suggest that anyone could require that an issue be considered by the appropriate

> court, rules have been enunciated by courts which confine the right to those persons possessing a certain interest in the issue.[1]

Originally, the test for determining the *locus standi* of a person depended upon the relief sought. For a person seeking declaratory or injunctive orders to have standing, it was required that the person must be a member of the public who suffers or is at risk of suffering particular direct and substantial damage other than, and different from, that which was common to all the rest of the public.[2] The rules relating to standing for the purpose of applying for the prerogative orders were expressed in various ways. With regard to *certiorari*, it was said that the applicant must be a person who is aggrieved or has a particular grievance.[3] A more restrictive rule for standing, however, applied to the prerogative order of *mandamus*. The test for this was that the applicant must have a sufficient interest,[4] or should be able to show that a legal specific right (i.e. a right recognised by statute or the common law) had been adversely affected.[5] In the latter instance, the applicant had to show a special damage or adverse detriment resulting from the invasion of a legal right or interest, and not merely a personal or economic interest.

This position changed in 1978 with the introduction of the *Rules of the Supreme Court* of England. Order 53 of these Rules (which is exactly the same as Order 16 of the *National Court Rules* (Ch 38) in Papua New Guinea) ostensibly discarded the technical limitations on *locus standi*. As a result, the different tests for determining *locus standi* were replaced by a single test for all forms of relief. The new test is the "sufficient interest" of the applicant in the matter to which the application relates.

The term "sufficient interest" has no specific definition in common law, and there is no great consistency or uniformity in its interpretation. While the English courts seem to use the term to mean "an aggrieved person",[6] or a person who has a "genuine concern or is genuinely

---

1 L A Stein (ed) *Locus Standi* (1979) 3.

2 Ref. *Boyce v Paddington Borough Council* [1903] 1 Ch 109.

3 Ref. *R v Thames Magistrates' Court; Ex parte Greenbaum* (1957) 55 LGR 129.

4 Ref. *R v Cotham* [1898] 1 QB 802.

5 Ref. *R v Guardians of Lewisham Union* [1897] 1 QB 498.

6 Ref. *R v Inland Revenue Commissioners; Ex parte National Federation of Self-Employed and Small Businesses Ltd* [1980] 2 All ER 378 at 389; [1980] QB 407 at 421; [1980] 2 WLR 579 at 585.

concerned",[7] other common law countries have used it interchangeably with "an adversely affected person", or a person with a "real interest", "personal interest", "personal stake or injury in the outcome of the controversy",[8] or "special interest".

One of the most notable attempts to define the term is Lord Denning's classic statement that "any 'person aggrieved' by the failure of a public authority to do its duty has a sufficient interest".[9] As to who is an aggrieved person, he said:

> ... I would endorse the general principle stated by Professor H W R Wade QC in his Administrative Law (4th Edn, 1977, p 608). He says that:
>
> > 'It [the law] should recognise that public authorities should be compellable to perform their duties, as a matter of public interest, at the instance of any person genuinely concerned; and in suitable cases, subject always to discretion, the court should be able to award the remedy on the application of a public-spirited citizen who has no other interest than regard for the due observance of the law.'[10]

He then elaborated on this general principle by applying it to the circumstances of the case thus:

> So I come back to the question: have these self-employed and small shopkeepers, through their association, a 'sufficient interest' to complain of this amnesty? Have they a genuine grievance? Are they genuinely concerned? Or are they mere busybodies? This matter is to be decided objectively. A 'busybody' is one who meddles officiously in other people's affairs. He convinces himself, subjectively, that there is cause for grievance when there is none. He should be refused. But a man who is genuinely concerned can point, objectively, to something that has gone wrong and should be put right. He should be heard.[11]

The main contribution of Lord Denning's objective test is the practical guide it provides with regard to the purpose of the sufficient interest test, namely, to filter applications for judicial review in order to limit interference with administrative actions to situations where a person has a genuine interest in a case. By barring busybodies from pursuing

---

7 *Ibid.*
8 *Baker v Carr* (1962) 369 US 186 at 204.
9 Above, note 6 at 389, 420 and 585, respectively.
10 *Id.*, pp. 390, 422 and 586, respectively.
11 *Id.*, pp. 391, 422 and 586, respectively.

doomed applications through the courts, the sufficient interest test ensures that the courts' time will not be occupied with frivolous or nuisance suits. However, notwithstanding this contribution, Lord Denning's definition does not tell us precisely the type of interests the law will recognise and what it would take to make the interests sufficient. On this point, Jacobs explains that the term is generally construed very liberally. According to him:

> The question of what is a 'sufficient interest' in the matter to which the application relates appears to be a mixed question of fact and law: a question of fact and degree and the relationship between the applicant and the matter to which the application relates, having regard to all the circumstances of the case. The term 'interest' should perhaps not be given a narrow construction, but should be regarded as including any connection, association or interrelation between the applicant and the matter to which the application relates.[12]

This suggests that there is no limit to the type of interests. Consequently, a variety of interests, including legal, equitable, property or proprietary, contractual, economic, commercial, business, financial, family, educational and even social and political interests, would all be legally acceptable interests for purposes of meeting the sufficient interest test.

It should be noted, however, that although the sufficient interest test may be construed liberally and is supposed to be generally applied to all the remedies, without any rigid adherence to the technical differences between the remedies, there are some indications that the nature of the relief sought may be a relevant factor in determining the standing of an applicant. In the view of Aldous and Alder:

> ... the standing requirement is at its most liberal in relation to *certiorari* followed, in descending order, by prohibition, *mandamus*, declaration and injunction. In the case of the injunction, because of the drastic nature of this remedy and the well-established body of law surrounding it, standing may be limited to a person whose legal or equitable rights are affected.[13]

With regard to the factors that determine the sufficiency of the interest, it would appear that that depends entirely on the discretion of the court. This is implicit in Lord Diplock's dictum that the flexibility of the term "leave[s] to the court an unfettered discretion to decide what in its own

---

12 I H Jacobs (ed) *The Supreme Court Practice* (1982) V 1, 875.

13 G Aldous and J Alder, *Applications for Judicial Review; Law and Practice* (London: Butterworths 1985) 95.

good judgment it considers to be a 'sufficient interest' on the part of an applicant in the particular circumstances of the case..."[14] For this reason, the issue as to what constitutes sufficient interest is regarded as a matter of judicial discretion that is exercised on the basis of the facts in every case and according to the legal principles developed by the courts.

Among the principles developed by the courts, the governing one is that applicants must show a *bona fide* connection between their interest and the substance of the complaint. As Lord Scarman puts it,

> The one legal principle, which is implicit in the case law and accurately reflected in the rules of court, is that in determining the sufficiency of an applicant's interest it is necessary to consider the matter to which the application relates. It is wrong in law ... for the court to attempt an assessment of the sufficiency of an applicant's interest without regard to the matter of his complaint.[15]

This principle is an attribute of the adversarial system of the English law of judicial review. It is, thus, premised upon the view that the primary function of the courts is to resolve disputes between private citizens and the State and not to control the administration. Consequently, a member of the public has no automatic access to the courts and must, therefore, show a *bona fide* connection with the case.

The second legal principle that is applied in determining whether or not an applicant for judicial review has a sufficient interest states that there is a distinction between a public interest suit and a private interest suit, and the requirements of sufficient interest are different in each case.[16] A private interest suit is an action brought by an individual or a group of individuals to assert their private rights or interests. Therefore, in order to obtain leave to apply for judicial review, these persons must show a *bona fide* connection between their interest and the substance of the complaint.

A public interest suit, on the other hand, is a legal action which is instituted by the Attorney-General in his role as guardian of the public interest in order to assert a public right. Private individuals cannot, on their own motion, institute a public interest suit. This is in accordance with a basic principle of English law that public rights are a matter for the Crown. The general rule is that the only way private individuals can institute action

---

14 *Inland Revenue Commissioners v National Federation of Self-Employed and Small Businesses Ltd* [1981] 2 All ER 93 at 105; [1982] AC 617 at 642; [1981] 2 WLR 722 at 738.
15 Per Lord Scarman, *Id.*, p 113, 653 and 748, respectively.
16 *Ibid.*

to assert a public right is by obtaining the Attorney-General's *fiat* or by requesting the Attorney-General to exercise the power to intervene on their behalf.[17] Also known as a relator action, this type of action is:

> ... one in which the Attorney-General, on the relation of individuals (who may include local authorities or companies) brings an action to assert a public right. It can properly be said to be a fundamental principle of English law that private rights can be asserted by individuals, but that public rights can only be asserted by the Attorney-General as representing the public. In terms of constitutional law, the rights of the public are vested in the Crown, and the Attorney-General enforces them as an officer of the Crown. And just as the Attorney-General has in general no power to interfere with the assertion of private rights, so in general no private person has the right of representing the public in the assertion of public rights. If he tries to do so his action can be struck out.[18]

If the Attorney-General intervenes at the request of the relators, the power to initiate such proceedings is not affected by whether or not the relators have standing in their own right.

The third and final legal principle that is applied by the English courts in determining whether or not an applicant for judicial review has a sufficient interest states that "[a]part from cases involving obvious busy bodies, the *locus standi* issue is closely interrelated with the substance of the case and must be decided at the full *inter partes* hearing".[19] This means that the issue as to whether a particular person or body is entitled to ask the court for relief is closely linked to the merits of the complaint that is being made. This principle emerged from the House of Lords' decision in *Inland Revenue Commissioners v National Federation of Self-Employed and Small Businesses Ltd*,[20] where it was held that the issue of *locus standi* is:

---

17 *Gouriet v Union of Post Office Workers* [1978] AC 435; [1977] All ER 70; [1977] 3 WLR 300. The exception to this general rule is that "A plaintiff can sue without joining the Attorney-General in two cases: first, where the interference with the public right is such as that some private right of his is at the same time interfered with (e.g., where an obstruction is so placed in a highway that the owner of premises abutting upon the highway is specially affected by reason that the obstruction interferes with his private right to access from and to his premises to and from the highway); and, secondly, where no private right is interfered with, but the plaintiff, in respect of his public right, suffers special damage peculiar to himself from the interference with the public right." Per Buckley J in *Boyce v Paddington Borough Council*, above, note 2 at 114.

18 Per Lord Wilberforce, above, note 17 at 477, 80 and 310, respectively.

19 Aldous and Alder, above, note 13 at 95.

20 Above, note 14.

> ... a 'threshold' question in the sense that the court must direct its mind to it and form a prima facie view about it on the material that is available at the first stage. The prima facie view so formed, if favourable to the applicant, may alter on further consideration in the light of further evidence that may be before the court at the second stage the hearing of the application for judicial review itself.[21]

The effect of this decision is that, notwithstanding the fact that an applicant has been granted leave, the question of the *locus standi* of the applicant remains open for the court to consider at all times and may properly be argued during the substantive hearing. Lord Fraser of Tullybelton, in his concurring judgment in the same case, emphasised the point when he said:

> I recognise that in some cases, perhaps in many, it may be impracticable to decide whether an applicant has a sufficient interest or not, without having evidence from both parties as to the matter to which the application relates, and that, in such cases, the court before whom the matter comes in the first instance cannot refuse leave to the applicant at the ex parte stage, under r 3(5). The court which grants leave at that stage will do so on the footing that it makes a provisional finding of sufficient interest, subject to revisal later on, and it is therefore not necessarily to be criticised merely because the final decision is that the applicant did not have sufficient interest. But where, after seeing the evidence of both parties, the proper conclusion is that the applicant did not have a sufficient interest to make the application, the decision ought to be made on that ground...[22]

The application of this principle has been interpreted to mean that *locus standi* is now effectively abolished as a separate requirement by merging it with the merits of the applicant's allegations. The better view, however, according to Aldous and Alder, is that:

> The merits of the applicant's allegations are at most one of several factors to be taken into account, and *locus standi* remains an analytically distinct matter, albeit depending upon the balancing of several factors, one of which is the gravity of the allegations.[23]

In their view, ultimately, taking into account the substance of the case, the governing criteria for determining the *locus standi* of an applicant are as follows:

1. The scope and purpose of the particular statutory power or duty is probably the single most important consideration. On this

---

21 Per Lord Diplock, *ibid.*

22 *Id.*, pp. 107, 645 and 741, respectively.

23 Aldous and Alder, above, note 13 at 94.

basis an applicant must show that he possesses an interest which as a matter of construction the governing legislation recognises.

2. The gravity of the allegations. Thus an applicant who fails the first test may have standing to challenge exceptionally serious governmental misdeeds.
3. The strength of the applicant's case.
4. The public interest in the governmental act challenged. For example, a decision involving, say, a major highway, or environmental conservation, is arguably challengeable by anyone, whether or not a resident of the affected area.
5. The nature of the remedy sought. The relief required by the applicant will sometimes be crucial. For example an applicant is more likely to obtain certiorari than mandamus if it cannot be shown that the particular statutory function is intended for his protection.
6. The nature of the applicant's injury. This is the traditional *locus standi* test. It is reasonably clear that an applicant whose legal rights in the strict sense are affected will rarely be turned away, although such a case is possible. Conversely, the absence of a legal right is no longer fatal...
7. Previous connection with the matter in hand. For example a person who has been permitted to appear at a public inquiry will have standing to challenge any subsequent decision.[24]

Application of the Doctrine in Papua New Guinea

In Papua New Guinea, there is no conceptual view of what the term sufficient interest means. The practice to date indicates that the courts have adopted a practical and convenient approach to determining the issue of *locus standi*. On the assumption that the meaning of the term is common knowledge, the courts normally take the meaning for granted and proceed directly to searching for material evidence to substantiate a finding of sufficient interest.[25] While this approach may have the advantage of being

---

24 *Id.*, p. 95.

25 Andrew J's decision in *PNG Air Pilots v Director of Civil Aviation* [1983] PNGLR 1 may be an exception. In that case, His Honour found that the applicants had sufficient interest because they had a "real interest" (based upon the objects of the PNG Air Pilots Association) in a matter that involved economic, contractual and other interests affecting their livelihoods and day to day working lives. To reach this conclusion, His Honour explained at p. 3 that *locus standi* "is a right to appear and ask for such an order (like a declaration)", and in order to have *locus*, the applicant

pragmatic, it arguably denies the law the analytical content that is necessary for a clear and consistent development.

1. *Bona Fide* Connection With the Case

Notwithstanding the absence of a conceptual notion of the meaning of the sufficient interest, there is clear evidence that most judges adopt a rather liberal interpretation of the term. Indeed, the term is generally considered as flexible enough to embrace any interest that establishes a bona fide connection or link between the applicant and the matter to which the application relates.

Thus, in *NTN Pty Ltd v PTC*,[26] Wilson J held that even though the applicant, holder of a television broadcasting licence, had no legal right infringed if the PTC, the licensing authority, acted lawfully in granting a licence to a competitor, the applicant's commercial interests were deemed to be so affected by the appearance of an alternative broadcaster that it was held to constitute a sufficient interest in the matter to which the application related.

In *Arawe Logging Pty Ltd v PNG*,[27] Brunton AJ, following the same approach, held that although the first plaintiff company was not a party to the contract enshrined in the Timber Rights Purchase Agreement between the second plaintiffs and the State, the company had a sufficient interest in the matter to which the application related to dispute the issue of the Timber Permit over this resource to another company because:

> ... it is an applicant for a Timber Permit. An applicant for a Timber Permit which may be granted or refused in the exercise of a ministerial discretion is quite clearly an interested party to the exercise of that discretion...*R. v. Hillingdon London Borough Council; Ex parte Royco Homes Ltd.* [1974] 1 QB 720 ... In addition, ... they are property-owners of the land over which the subject Timber Rights Purchase Agreement

---

must show "actual or apprehended injury or damage to his property or proprietary rights, to his business or economic interests and perhaps to his social or political interests". This decision was adopted and applied by the Supreme Court in *Mamun Investments Pty Ltd v Ponda* [1995] PNGLR 1; SC490. However, it was not a judicial review case, and the decision was handed down before the *National Court Rules* came into force.

26 [1987] PNGLR 70.

27 [1988-89] PNGLR 216; (1989) N751.

> and the Timber Permits have been issued, and applicants for a Timber Permit.[28]

In a brief statement explaining the sufficient interest test, His Honour pointed out that:

> Property is one of the most important *indicia* of interest in the ascertainment of locus standi. Property owners who have had their property-rights adversely altered because of the exercise of an administrative discretion are clearly persons aggrieved...[29]

The decision in *NCDIC v Crusoe Pty Ltd*[30] best illustrates the range of interests that the courts would recognise and the unlimited flexibility of the connection required between an applicant and the case to meet the test of sufficient interest. In that case, Brunton J found that the NCDIC had no property rights in Lot 29, the land which was the subject matter of the application. Nevertheless, he held that the Commission had a sufficient interest in the matter to which the application related to seek a review of the decision of the Minister to approve the grant of a lease to the respondent. The Commission's interest in this case was based on fact, law and a legal fiction. The factual basis was the Commission's occupation of the land at the material time that the proceedings were instituted. The legal basis was the Commission's legal status as a statutory body with powers "to control, manage and administer the National Capital District and to ensure the welfare of the ... District and of the persons in it."[31] Finally, the Commission's interest was based on the fact that it was an applicant for a special purpose lease to Lot 29 and, even though it had not been granted the lease, it had a "legitimate expectation" that it would eventually be granted the lease. Incidentally, the decision of the Court placed considerable weight on this legal fiction. As His Honour explained:

> ... if a legitimate expectation can be said to arise where an authority has promised a certain cause of action, there would be no reason why an expectation could not arise by default, by omission, if as a result of the default or omission, the party relying on the default or omission could have reasonably expected that it would get what it wanted and it acted openly in a manner consistent with that expectation, and the authority

28 *Id.*, p. 7. See also *Amadio Pty Ltd v PNG* [1992] PNGLR 218, where the Court held that the applicant for leave had a sufficient interest because it had applied for prospecting authority over land which was the subject of the decision that was being challenged and further that it was a company owned by persons who claimed to have an interest according to custom in the land.

29 Above, note 27 at 4-5.

30 [1993] PNGLR 139.

31 Ref. *National Capital District Government (Preparatory Arrangements) Act* (Ch 392) section 10.

> was aware or should have been aware of that conduct. Such a rule is both appropriate and applicable to the circumstances of Papua New Guinea because of the notoriety of inefficiency within the public sector, which can so often damage individual rights, but it needs to be administered with good conscience, equity, fairness, reasonableness, and justice.
> Accordingly, I find that the NCDIC had a legitimate expectation that it would get a lease over Lot 29, and that it was only the incompetence of the Lands Department that prevented this expectation from being materialised into a right: a lease.[32]

Of course, it is clear that this decision was largely influenced by His Honour's perception of the poor work ethics of the public sector. Apart from that, the significance of the decision lies in the rather ingenious application of the doctrine of legitimate expectation (which had hitherto been restricted to only migration cases) as a device to substantiate a finding of sufficient interest. At the same time, the somewhat ambiguous argument that a legitimate expectation could arise by default or omission (i.e. without an explicit promise that the NCDIC would be granted a lease) illustrates the difficulties that the courts may sometimes face in the absence of a conceptual notion or authoritative definition of the term "sufficient interest".

Nonetheless, all these cases illustrate the type of interests the courts will recognise and how liberal the courts have been in applying the sufficient interest test. As indicated, the procedure adopted in all the cases shows that the determination of the issue is regarded as a mixed question of fact and law. Depending on the evidence available to the courts, the courts look for the existence, or otherwise, of a *bona fide* connection (i.e. interest) of the applicant with the case and then exercise their discretion as to whether or not the connection is genuine enough to be considered sufficient. It is, therefore, a fair assessment to say that the courts in Papua New Guinea have adopted the principle that applicants must show a *bona fide* connection between their interest and the substance of the complaint. In applying the principle, consistent with the English practice, the Papua New Guinea courts have also adopted a liberal attitude towards the type of interests that would meet the sufficient interest test.

The only notable exception to this prevailing liberal attitude is the decision of Amet J (as he then was) in *Mugridge v Minister for Labour and*

32 Above, note 30 at 158.

Employment.[33] This case arose out of the refusal by the Secretary of the Department of Labour and Employment, pursuant to the *Employment of Non-Citizens Act* (Ch 374), to grant a work permit to the plaintiff's prospective employer. Under the Act, employers of non-citizens are permitted to apply for a work permit, but the Secretary of the Department has a discretion to grant or refuse the permit. The Act also provides for a right of appeal against a refusal by the Secretary to the Minister and, significantly, confers this right not only on the applicant employers but on "any person aggrieved by a decision of the Secretary". On the strength of this provision, the plaintiff employee himself appealed to the Minister. Following the Minister's dismissal of the appeal, the plaintiff brought this action seeking leave to apply for a review of the Minister's decision. The issue before the Court was whether or not the applicant had sufficient interest in the matter to which the application related to invoke the judicial review jurisdiction of the Court. Without reference to any authority, Amet J (as he then was) held that the plaintiff did not have sufficient interest in the matter because "he does not have any legal or constitutional right or standing to seek redress from this Court". According to him:

> The legal position is that the application is not that of such an intending non-citizen employee but that of the intending employer. *The intending employee in reality is outside of the jurisdiction, and does not have any legal or constitutional right or standing to seek redress from this Court.* If, as ought strictly to be the case, such an intending non-citizen employee is outside of Papua New Guinea and the application for work permit is made by the intending employer, then that intending employee loses nothing if the application is refused. *He has no right, legal or constitutional in the first instance.* The right to grant or not to grant a work permit is a sovereign right of this Independent Nation and *the decision of the Minister is final and there is no legal or constitutional interest on the part of the intending employee that needs to be reviewed by any court in this jurisdiction.*
>
> The application for leave therefore is refused.[34]

Soon after this decision was handed down, the PNG Law Society published a commentary on it. In a scathing attack on the decision, the Law Society referred to it as "a significant impediment to the further expansion of [the jurisdiction of the National and Supreme Courts to

---

33 [1987] PNGLR 348.

34 *Id.*, at 351. (Emphasis added.)

review administrative decisions]".[35] The following passage, quoted, *in extenso*, from the commentary of the Law Society, provides an interesting and accurate insight into the law:

> In the first place the decision appears to misunderstand the nature of the relief available in applications for judicial review. Certainly, the right to grant or not to grant a work permit is one for the discretion of the Minister, and an applicant cannot complain if the Minister decides against an application, provided the Minister has made his decision according to law. An applicant or other person aggrieved by a refusal is given a right to appeal and, according to ordinary principles of public law, the Minister must decide the appeal in accordance with normal requirements, namely, he must only take into account relevant considerations, he must not be biased, he must not act unreasonably. It is the right to have the appeal determined according to law - a right given by s. 7(5) of the Act - which is asserted in and protected by an application for judicial review - not a right to insist that the public official exercise his discretion in a particular manner. Provided the decision is lawful, the fact that it is unfavourable is no ground for complaint.
>
> Accordingly, even if it is true to say that an applicant must establish some legal right before he can satisfy O 16 r 3(5), then the right to have his appeal under s 7(5) determined lawfully must satisfy that requirement.
>
> But the case is more important not so much for its consideration of the effect of Sections 6 and 7 of the *Employment of Non-Citizens Act* but because it has revived in Papua New Guinea what was described by Lord Scarman in the English House of Lords decision of *Inland Revenue Commissioners v National Federation of Self-Employed and Small Businesses Ltd* as the 'heresy' that an applicant must establish 'a legal specific right to ask for the interference of the Court' before an application for judicial review can be heard. That heresy was described in that case by Lord Scarman as a 'deplorable' decision and was soundly put to rest by each of the five members of the House of Lords in determining the meaning of the identical English provision to O 16 r 3(5).
>
> ... By holding that an applicant must be able to show an infringement of some legal right before the power of judicial review can be invoked, the decision, in the writer's submission, constitutes a significant, and unfortunate, restriction on the field of persons entitled to seek the assistance of the Courts to review administrative action... The effect of the judgment in Mugridge's case is to deprive the legislative formula 'sufficient interest' of any of the width intended by its authors and to

---

35 *Law Tok* (Boroko: PNG Law Society June 1989) 17.

> replace it with a rigid and restrictive test of 'legal or constitutional' right. Surely the purpose of O 16 r 3(5) is to give the Court a wide discretion to allow applications by persons with serious and genuine grievances, albeit no legal rights but to enable it to exclude from the process mere busy bodies whose interests are only academic or superficial. To tie the hands of the Court with prescriptions such as 'legal or constitutional' right is to undermine this beneficial discretion. If followed the new test will significantly dilute the power of the Courts to act as an effective guard against unfettered administrative and executive action by limiting access to the Courts to complain about that action to only those who can satisfy the qualification of 'legal or constitutional' right.[36]

In its concluding statement, the PNG Law Society expressed the hope that the Supreme Court would shortly get an opportunity to express its views on the meaning of the sufficient interest test in Order 16 Rule 3(5).

To date, the Supreme Court has not been presented with this opportunity. However, to my knowledge, the decision in *Mugridge v Minister for Labour and Employment* has not been cited in any case as support for an argument on the issue. Of course, it may be argued that the fact that the decision is ignored by subsequent cases does not overrule it, nor does it relegate the case to absolute oblivion. Therefore, its potential for distorting the systematic development of the law cannot be ruled out entirely. Hence, until the Supreme Court has the opportunity to rule on the issue, it might be a better approach for subsequent National Court cases on the issue to refer to it and provide reasons for not following it.

Having established that the courts generally apply the sufficient interest test rather liberally, the next question is whether the liberal construction of the test removes the differentiation based upon the remedies or the nature of the relief sought. In *PNG Air Pilots v Director of Civil Aviation*[37], Andrew J expressed the view that the requirements for *locus standi* of an applicant for judicial review varied according to the remedies sought. As he put it,

> ... depending on the nature of the relief which he seeks, a plaintiff will in general have a *locus standi* when he can show actual or apprehended injury or damage to his property or proprietary rights, to his business or economic interests and perhaps to his social or political interests. (Per Mason J in *Australian Conservation Foundation Inc v Commonwealth of Australia* (1980) 146 CLR 493; 54 ALJR 176), and as his Honour

36 *Id.*, at 18-19.
37 Above, note 25.

> said in *Robinson v The Western Australian Museum* (1977) 138 CLR 283 at 327-328:
>
> > 'The cases are infinitely various and so much depends in a given case on the nature of the relief which is sought, for what is a sufficient interest in one case may be less than sufficient interest in another.'[38]

This case, however, as indicated above, was not a judicial review case and, at any rate, was decided before the *National Court Rules* came into force. Since the passage of the Rules, there is no indication that the approach advocated here has been followed in any case. On the contrary, the courts have consistently applied the sufficient interest test generally to all the remedies without any reference to the differences between the remedies. This variation from the English practice, which still puts some weight on the differences between the remedies, shows that the application of the sufficient interest test in Papua New Guinea may be even more liberal than in the English courts.

2. Private v Public Interest Suits

The question as to whether or not the principle relating to the distinction between a public interest suit and a private interest suit is applicable in Papua New Guinea was heatedly debated in the celebrated case of *SCR No 4 of 1980; Re Petition of Somare*[39] (hereafter, the Somare case). This was a reference to the Supreme Court by the National Court, pursuant to section 18(2) of the *Constitution*. The main issue before the Court was whether the Leader of the Opposition in the National Parliament had legal standing to present a petition to the National Court disputing the validity of the *Defence Force (Presence Abroad) Act* (Ch 372). The Court unanimously agreed that the English principle pertaining to a relator action was not applicable in Papua New Guinea. On the issue of the *locus standi* of the petitioner, while Kidu CJ held that the citizenship of the petitioner gave him standing to challenge the Act, the two other judges, Kapi and Miles JJ, were of the opinion that something more than citizenship was required. In this instance, the two judges were ready to accept the

38 *Id.*, at 3.
39 [1981] PNGLR 265.

petitioner's position as a Member of Parliament and Leader of the Opposition as sufficient basis for the standing of the petitioner to invoke the powers of the Court to determine the constitutionality (or otherwise) of the *Defence Force (Presence Abroad) Act* (Ch 372).

There is no doubt that the decision in this case is remarkable for the part it played in the development of the underlying law. Clearly, the Supreme Court had not only discharged its constitutional duty of formulating a new rule in circumstances where there was no existing one on a point of law, but it had also demonstrated a bold judicial initiative and creativity. However, the extent to which the case may be cited as an authority today on the issue of the Order 16 requirement of sufficient interest is rather limited. This is because, in the first place, the case was decided before the *National Court Rules* (Ch 38) came into force. Hence, it may be argued that the decision was not based upon the sufficient interest test laid down by Order 16 of the *National Court Rules* (Ch 38).[40]

This argument may, of course, be countered by the fact that Kapi J (as he then was), in his concurring opinion, had referred specifically to the test by name and discussed its application within the context of the English common law. Another limiting factor is the fact that, at the time that the case was decided, the office of the Attorney-General had not yet been established in Papua New Guinea. Today, the country has an Attorney-General, an office which was established under the *Attorney-General Act 1989*. The authority of the decision in the Somare case may, therefore, be validly questioned in the light of the subsequent developments.

Even if all the above factors are discounted, it must be noted that the decision in the Somare case, nonetheless, has very limited impact on the law pertaining to *locus standi* in a public interest suit. The reason for this is that, notwithstanding the fact that the Court rejected the application of the English principle that public rights can only be asserted by the Attorney-General, the Court restricted its decision to situations involving only the constitutionality or otherwise of an Act of Parliament. In other words, if a person attempted today to bring a public interest suit to challenge an administrative act, the decision in the Somare case cannot be

---

40 The issue of the *locus standi* of a private person in a public interest suit was again raised in *Donigi v PNG* [1991] PNGLR 376. Even though reference was made to the Somare case, this case was not an application for judicial review. Consequently, the decision was not based upon the Order 16 requirement of a sufficient interest.

relied upon as an authority, since the decision is an authority for only the issue of the *locus standi* to challenge the constitutionality or otherwise of an Act of Parliament.[41]

Since the establishment of the office of Attorney-General, there has not been any case, to my knowledge, in which the Attorney-General's *fiat* has been invoked pursuant to the *Attorney-General Act.* The legal position regarding the applicability of the principle that requires a distinction between a public interest suit and a private interest suit, therefore, cannot be authoritatively stated. However, the decision in *SC Review No 9 of 1990: Application of Attorney-General*[42] throws some light on the point and indicates the direction in which the future legal development is likely to go. This case arose out of committal proceedings in the Boroko District Court against Mr Eliakim T ToBolton, the Managing Director of the Investment Corporation of Papua New Guinea, for charges brought by the Ombudsman Commission. Following the District Court's finding of a *prima facie* case, Mr ToBolton applied for judicial review of the Court's decision on the ground that the National Investment Authority did not come within the jurisdiction of the Ombudsman Commission and, therefore, the summons was invalid and unenforceable. The National Court upheld the argument that the National Investment Authority did not come within the jurisdiction of the Ombudsman Commission and, therefore, the District Court had no power to entertain the committal proceedings. Consequently, the committal orders were declared *ultra vires.*

Four months after the National Court's decision, i.e., after the expiration of the forty days permitted for lodging appeals under the *Supreme Court Act*, the Attorney-General brought the action in this case, applying for leave to apply for judicial review of the National Court's decision pursuant to section 155(2)(b) of the *Constitution.* The Attorney-General brought this action because, as he pointed out, the Public Prosecutor had failed to lodge an appeal from the National Court decision.

41 Ref *Skate v Chan* OS 468 of 1994. The plaintiff (the former Speaker of the National Parliament) sought a declaration in the National Court that the constitutional procedures necessary for the election of the defendant as Prime Minister were not followed and, consequently, the election of the defendant was invalid. With regard to the question of the *locus standi* of the plaintiff, the Court relied on the Somare case to rule that, by reason of being a citizen, the plaintiff had standing.

42 [1991] PNGLR 239.

He brought the action on the belief that section 7(c) of the *Attorney-General Act*[43] empowered him to intervene without the need to comply with requirements of a section 155(2)(b) review. The issues before the Supreme Court were, first, whether the Attorney-General had standing to apply for judicial review and, secondly, whether this was an appropriate case in which a judicial review should be granted.

On the issue of the standing of the Attorney-General, since this ground was not argued before the Court, the Court simply noted, after reviewing the relevant legislation, that the Attorney-General had no prosecution function and, therefore, could not have standing to bring the action. The Court's reason for refusing leave was that the applicant had not satisfied the established criteria[44] for seeking leave to apply for judicial review under section 155(2)(b) of the *Constitution*. In the opinion of the Court:

> .... the applicant has misconceived the nature of both a judicial review under s 155(2)(b) of the *Constitution* and relator proceedings which may be commenced by the Attorney-General. They are two distinct proceedings. With respect, the present case is not one of a relator proceedings. This is not a case in which the Attorney-General is seeking to enforce the law or to protect public rights: see, eg, *Attorney-General; Ex rel McWhirter v Independent Broadcasting Authority* [1973] QB 629. Even if the Attorney-General had standing and may be regarded as a party aggrieved by the decision of the National Court, he is still required to satisfy the requirements of s 155(2)(b) of the *Constitution*, as interpreted in earlier decisions which have involved a consideration of that provision. In considering that issue, s 7(c) [of the *Attorney-General Act*] is of no assistance to the Attorney-General.[45]

The inference that may be drawn from this opinion is that, following the enactment of the *Attorney-General Act*, the English principle pertaining to a relator action is now applicable in Papua New Guinea. This means that the courts in Papua New Guinea may also accept the principle that there is a distinction between a public interest suit and a private interest suit and may, therefore, vary the requirements of *locus standi* accordingly. If

---

43 This section provides, *inter alia,* that "The duties, functions and responsibilities of the Attorney-General are ... (c) to exercise the functions vested in the Office of Attorney-General by virtue of the underlying law including the bringing of proceedings known as relator proceedings".
44 The established criteria is that "the onus is on the applicant to show that there are cogent and convincing reasons and exceptional circumstances where some substantial injustice is manifest or the case is of special gravity and the applicant must justify why his right of appeal was not exercised and allowed to expire." Above, note 42 at 241.
45 Per Kapi DCJ. *Id.*, at 241-242.

this inference is correct, then the current practice in Papua New Guinea may be said to be exactly the same as in the English common law and, as indicated by the Supreme Court opinion quoted above, the courts in Papua New Guinea are likely to rely on the English authorities to interpret and clarify the application of the principle. It should be emphasised, however, that since the inference about the applicability of the principle is derived from an *obiter dictum*, our conclusion about the legal position is still subject to an authoritative judicial pronouncement.

3. *Locus* and Substance

A review of the decisions on *locus standi* shows that, procedurally, the issue of *locus standi* is regarded as a threshold question to be determined at the leave stage. Hence, unless contested in an appeal against the decision on leave, the issue is normally considered during the leave stage and hardly ever raised at the full hearing.[46] Does this mean that the principle which states that the *locus standi* issue is closely interrelated with the substance of the case and must be decided at the full *inter partes* hearing does not apply in Papua New Guinea?

In *Ombudsman Commission v Donohoe,*[47] the Supreme Court ruled that the courts are not required at the preliminary stage of applying for leave to hear arguments relating to the substantive matter of the case. According to Amet J (as he then was),

> On an application for leave to file an application for judicial review, the Court need only be satisfied as to the requirements of O 16, rr 2, 3 and 5. The application, of course, is ex parte and so the Court does not have any other material contesting the application. The Court is not required to address the matters specified in O 16, r 1(2). These are matters for consideration by the Court hearing the substantive application. I consider that the substantial issues raised are matters properly to be considered by the Court hearing the substantive

46 The only exception to this practice occurred in *Olei v Provincial Land Court at Port Moresby* [1984] PNGLR 295, one of the first cases to apply the sufficient interest test under Order 16. In this case, the issue of the sufficient interest of the applicant was raised again during the substantive trial. McDermott J allowed the interjection, heard arguments on the issue and ruled on it. The practice, however, has not been followed in any other case.

47 [1985] PNGLR 348.

> application, depending on its conclusion of facts upon an assessment of all the evidence and the benefit of legal arguments.[48]

Since the established practice in Papua New Guinea is to consider the issue of *locus standi* during the *ex parte* proceeding of an application for leave, does the Supreme Court's injunction to reserve the substantive issues of an application for the full hearing prevent linking the issue of *locus standi* to the substance of the case? Of course, in an *ex parte* proceeding, a court may not have any material contesting the application. Yet that does not necessarily rule out the possibility of the substance (i.e. merits or demerits) of the applicant's allegations having a bearing on the decision to grant or refuse leave. The cases on judicial review in Papua New Guinea are replete with numerous instances of judges basing their decisions on leave on the merits or demerits of the case.[49] Indeed, notwithstanding the ostensible protest by Amet J (as he then was) against taking into account the substance of the case at the leave stage, it is not unusual to find some of His Honour's own decisions on leave applications based on the merits of the allegation.[50]

Nonetheless, considering the substance of the case at the leave stage does not necessarily mean that the *locus standi* issue is closely interrelated with the substance of the case. A close study of the practice and procedure in the National Court indicates that the determination of the *locus standi* of an applicant is independent of whether or not the substantive issues of the case have any merit. Andrew J made this point abundantly clear when he stated that:

> I am not here deciding if, in fact, the actions of the Minister or of the Committee of Review were harsh and oppressive but whether, on an objective assessment of the evidence available, the plaintiff has a sufficient interest in the matter and that the issues raised are substantial ...[51]

48 *Id.*, at 361. This decision has recently been affirmed by the Supreme Court in the case of *Geno v PNG* [1993] PNGLR 22.

49 Ref. *Sigulogo v Leadership Tribunal* (1990) N829; *Vanderlist v Mount Hagen Golf Club* [1990] PNGLR 315; and *Application of Gigimat,* [1992] PNGLR 322.

50 The best illustrations of this are his decisions in *Mugridge v Minister for Labour and Employment*, above, note 33; and *Geno v PNG*, above, note 48.

51 *Valentine v Somare* [1988-89] PNGLR 51 at 55. Cf., however, the following views of Miles J in the earlier Somare case. In his concurring opinion in that case, His Honour expressed the following view on the correlation between *locus standi* and the substance of the case: "... I see merit in regarding the consideration of standing as part of the merits of the case itself. Gibbs J, as he then was, has referred to the situation where it may be a relatively simple matter to uphold the

Accordingly, even where the merits or demerits of the substantive issues are taken into account at the leave stage, the distinction is, nevertheless, made between the standing of the applicant and the substance of the case. In order to emphasise this distinctness, the courts are very careful to separate the two issues by considering the substance of the case under a separate legal issue, namely, whether or not the applicant has an arguable case. It is, therefore, incorrect and misleading to state, as Naru does, that "Other rights such as a right to be accorded natural justice (e.g. *Gegeyo v Minister for Lands and Physical Planning* [1987] PNGLR 331) or to be treated fairly (e.g. Re *Application of NCDIC* [1987] PNGLR 339) would amount to sufficient interest for purposes of judicial review".[52] The right to be accorded a hearing or to be fairly treated are legal issues which, if violated, are substantive matters, as Amet J pointed out, to be properly considered during the substantive hearing. At the leave stage, these matters may be relevant in determining whether or not the applicant has an arguable case, but that, as Andrew J explained above, is entirely independent of the question of standing. Wilson J's decision in *NTN Pty Ltd v PTC*,[53] reinforces this point and illustrates the order in which the two issues are to be considered. In that case, he explained that:

> Applications for leave for judicial review involve the exercise of discretion. Such discretion must be exercised judicially. Once a court is satisfied that the applicant has sufficient interest (O 16, r 3(5)) it then exercises its discretion as to whether leave should be granted. This discretion is embodied in O 16, r 3(1).
>
> *In exercising its discretion the court must consider whether the applicant has an arguable case.* In *Inland Revenue Commissioners v National Federation of Self-Employed and Small Businesses Ltd* [1982]

---

constitutional validity of legislation without embarking on questions relating to standing which may present complex issues of fact and more difficult issues of law: *Robinson v Western Australian Museum* (1977) 51 ALJR 806 at p. 831. In other words it would be preferable if standing in constitutional matters was not decided until the facts were established, the legislation properly examined and the case as a whole fully argued. The court is capable of protecting itself against frivolous applications." (Above, note 39 at 311). These views are, however, not binding since they were *obiter dicta* from a non-judicial review decision that was handed down before Order 16 came into force.

52 K Naru, "*Locus Standi* Applications for Judicial Review" in R W James and I Fraser (eds), *Legal Issues in a Developing Society* (Port Moresby: Faculty of Law, University of Papua New Guinea 1992) 56-68 at 59.

53 Above, note 26.

> AC 617, Lord Diplock set out the principles upon which the Court should act and I respectfully adopt them. Lord Diplock said (at 644):
>
> > 'If, on a quick perusal of the material then available, the court (that is the Judge who first considers the application for leave) *thinks that it discloses what might on further consideration turn out to be an arguable case* in favour of granting to the applicant the relief claimed, it ought, in the exercise of a judicial discretion, to give him leave to apply for the relief. The discretion that the court is exercising at this stage is not the same as that which it is called upon to exercise when all the evidence is in and the matter has been fully argued at the hearing of the application. (My emphasis.)'[54]

This clear difference between the principles for determining sufficient interest and an arguable case shows that, although the courts in Papua New Guinea, like their counterparts in the English common law, consider the issue of *locus* as an analytically distinct matter, the principle which states that the *locus standi* issue is closely interrelated with the substance of the case may not be applicable in Papua New Guinea.

Reform Proposals

The application of the *locus standi* doctrine in Papua New Guinea shows that, although not often articulated, there are two basic legal principles that are operative and underlie all decisions on the issue. The first states that, in order to have a sufficient interest to apply for judicial review, there must exist a *bona fide* connection or link between the applicant and the matter to which an application relates. The term sufficient interest is construed liberally and generally applied to all the remedies without any rigid adherence to the technical differences between the remedies. The second principle requires that a distinction be made between a public interest suit and a private interest suit, with the requirements of *locus standi* varying according to the type of suit. Both principles are applied virtually in the same way as the English common law courts do. A third principle, which states that the *locus standi* issue is closely interrelated with the substance of the case and must be decided at the full *inter partes* hearing, though applied by the English common law courts, does not seem to be applicable in Papua New Guinea.

---

54 *Id.*, at 74. (Emphasis added.)

Having ascertained the principles that underlie the determination of *locus standi*, the crucial question remains whether the uncertainty that presently surrounds the issue of *locus standi* can be removed by this knowledge of the applicable principles. In other words, does the knowledge of the relevant principles make it any easier for a lawyer, for instance, to be able to better predict whether an applicant for judicial review will be deemed to have *locus standi* before a judicial determination of the issue? Under the current position of the law, it would appear that that is not likely to be the case. As indicated in the cases analysed above, even though the sufficient interest test may be liberally interpreted, judges sometimes have to strain to find cogent reasons to support a finding of sufficient interest, as happened in *NCDIC v Crusoe Pty Ltd*[55] This suggests that there may be lingering problems with the present position of the law which militate against the predictability of the law and, therefore, need to be reformed.

The first area of the law regarding standing that can benefit from reform is the clarification or ascertainment of the meaning of the term sufficient interest. In the absence of any authoritative judicial pronouncement on the meaning of the term, a statutory definition, as the case of *Olei v Provincial Land Court at Port Moresby*[56] shows, might be the answer.

In that case, although the applicant was not a party to the proceedings that gave rise to the decision of the Provincial Land Court at Port Moresby, he applied for leave to apply for judicial review of that decision. He contended that, notwithstanding the fact that he had previously given notice to that court of his interest and his desire to be heard, the two clans that he represented and who occupied part of the disputed land had never been notified of the hearing date of the Provincial Land Court proceedings. Although the applicant was granted leave to apply for judicial review, the question of the *locus standi* of the applicant to maintain the action was raised again on the facts during the substantive trial. In deciding whether the plaintiff had a sufficient interest or not to apply for judicial review under Order 16, McDermott J, relying on *In re Portion 56 Morobe*,[57]

55 Above, note 30.
56 Above, note 46.
57 [1971-72] PNGLR 442.

pointed out that, under the *Land Disputes Settlement Act* (Ch 45), a person need not be a party to the earlier proceedings in order to be aggrieved. He explained the interest of the applicant in the matter as follows:

> All the applicant can say is: 'I am not a party to these proceedings, but I claim an interest in the land, the subject of the proceedings. I ask that the ownership order of the land court be quashed as it acted without jurisdiction. This may enable me in some way to be heard in another court or tribunal which has jurisdiction to determine ownership.'[58]

On the basis of this, he held that,

> It was submitted that I view a person with 'sufficient interest' as a 'person aggrieved'. These later words appear in s 55(1) of the *Land Disputes Settlement Act* whereby such a person may appeal a local land court decision to the District Land Court. It is because Mr Olei is aggrieved by the decision that he has sufficient interest to bring the present action.[59]

The clear lesson from this case is that the guidance offered by statute as to the class of persons who are intended to be considered as having an interest in a particular matter can greatly reduce, if not completely eradicate, the uncertainty that presently characterises the determination of a sufficient interest. Without in any way restricting the discretion of the court, it is possible, as this and other cases[60] show, that the statutory provision relating to a "person aggrieved" tremendously facilitated the determination of the issue of *locus standi*. By relying on the legislative intent evidenced in the *Land Disputes Settlement Act* (Ch 45), the court is provided with instant cogent reasons to support its decision. This makes the meaning of sufficient interest clearer and more settled and also removes the temptation to fall into the kind of errors that occurred in the Mugridge case. The guidance offered by statutory provision can, thus, provide the basis for the development of more settled and consistent rules of law and practice regarding the determination of *locus standi*.

Yet another area of the law that, in my view, can benefit from reform is the current practice of distinguishing between a public interest suit and a private interest suit for the purposes of determining *locus standi*. This distinction should be abolished and replaced with a uniform procedure and

---

58 Above, note 46 at 298.

59 *Ibid.*

60 Ref *R v Inland Revenue Commissioners; Ex parte National Federation of Self-Employed and Small Businesses Ltd*, above, note 6. In that case, Lord Denning admitted that his definition of the term sufficient interest was guided by "what many statutes have done in similar situations".

standard of sufficient interest for all judicial review applications. The basis of this proposal is that the historical reasons that justify the distinction between a public interest suit and a private interest suit in England are hardly relevant in the particular circumstances of Papua New Guinea. Besides, the strongest argument that has been used so far to justify the adoption of the practice, "the figment about floods of litigation" if the requirements for standing are relaxed, as I have shown elsewhere,[61] is not supported by any empirical evidence in Papua New Guinea. The final reason is best expressed in the words of Kidu CJ. As he eloquently put it in the Somare case:

> The People, depository of all powers in Papua New Guinea, have, through the *Constitution*, directed that the Parliament make laws which comply with the *Constitution*. If the legislative power is exercised contrary to the *Constitution*, why should not the People come to this Court and complain? After all it is their power and they are, in my view, entitled to complain to the Supreme Court, in whom their power to determine the constitutionality or otherwise of an Act of the Parliament, is vested. As a beneficiary in trust is entitled to invoke the powers of the courts to ensure that the trustees act in their interest so should the People whose legislative power the Parliament exercises, complain to this Court if they think the Legislature acts contrary to the *Constitution* through which their power has been given to it.[62]

These words of wisdom send a powerful message in favour of relaxing the rules of *locus standi*. The logic and import of the message is that the distinction between a public interest suit and a private interest suit in Papua New Guinea, and the restriction that is consequently placed upon private individuals who may want to institute public interest suits, are, thus, not only anachronisms but may as well be unconstitutional.

---

61 Ref M A Ntumy, "Applications for Leave to Apply for Judicial Review: An Overview of a Decade's Applications" (1994) 22 *MLJ* 103-138.
62 Above, note 39 at 273.

CHAPTER 8

UNDUE DELAY

Apart from the requirement of sufficient interest, the only other criterion for determining whether to grant or refuse leave that is specifically mentioned in Order 16 is the time limit for bringing an application. This criterion is expressed in Rule 4 of Order 16 as follows:

> (1) Subject to this Rule, where in any case the Court considers that there has been *undue delay* in making an application for judicial review or, in a case to which sub-rule (2) applies, the application for leave under Rule 3 is made after the relevant period has expired, *the Court may refuse to grant* --
>
> (a) *leave for the making of the application; or*
>
> (b) any relief sought on the application,
>
> if, in the opinion of the Court, the granting of the relief sought would be likely to cause *substantial hardship to, or substantially prejudice the rights of, any person or would be detrimental to good administration.*
>
> (2) In the case of an application for an order of *certiorari* to remove any judgment, order, conviction or other proceeding for the purpose of quashing it, the relevant period for the purpose of sub-rule (1) is four months after the date of the proceeding.
>
> (3) Sub-rule (1) is without prejudice to any statutory provision which has the effect of limiting the time within which an application for judicial review may be made.[1]

The principle of delay enunciated in these provisions requires two distinct issues to be taken into account in granting an application for leave. The first one is the issue of "undue delay". The second one is the effect of granting the relief sought; whether this is "likely to cause substantial hardship to, or prejudice the rights of, any person or would be detrimental to good administration". This means that, under Order 16, "undue delay" *per se* does not justify a refusal of an application for leave. After the Court considers that there has been an "undue delay" in bringing an application, it has a further obligation to consider whether granting the application would

---

[1] (Emphasis added.)

be "likely to cause substantial hardship to, or prejudice the rights of, any person or would be detrimental to good administration".

Wilson J highlighted the importance of separating these two legal issues in *NTN Pty Ltd v PTC*.[2] After ruling that there had been "undue delay", His Honour made it clear that:

> The next issue for me to consider, having found undue delay, is whether the granting of the relief sought would cause substantial hardship, or substantially prejudice the rights of, any person or would be detrimental to good administration...
>
> On all of the material before me I am of the clear opinion that granting of the relief sought would be likely to cause substantial hardship to Media Niugini...[and] would also be detrimental to good administration.[3]

Thus, it is only after the court determines, on the basis of evidence available to it, that as a result of "undue delay" in bringing the application, the effect of granting the relief sought is "likely to cause substantial hardship to, or prejudice the rights of, any person or would be detrimental to good administration" that it may refuse to grant leave.

The decision of Doherty AJ to refuse leave in *Ex parte Gurupa*[4] is, therefore, open to question on the ground that it was based upon a finding of only "undue delay" without any consideration of the second issue of whether granting the relief sought was "likely to cause substantial hardship to, or prejudice the rights of, any person or would be detrimental to good administration".

How the Courts Determine Undue Delay

Except for applications in which the relief sought is an order of *certiorari* (where the time limit for instituting legal proceedings is fixed at four months from the date of the proceedings being challenged), Order 16 does not prescribe any specific time limit for bringing an application for leave. It simply confers a discretion on the Court to refuse to grant leave if it considers that there has been "undue delay" in making the application. In fact, even if an application for leave in which the relief sought is an order of *certiorari* is brought later than the four months stipulated in Rule 4(2),

---

[2] [1987] PNGLR 70.
[3] *Id.*, p. 76.
[4] (1990) N856.

that does not automatically defeat the action. The Court still has a discretion to grant or refuse to grant the order. As Doherty AJ expressed it:

> Although the current *National Court Rules* state that the four months is 'the relevant period' in considering whether there has been undue delay, it is not a mandatory period and the new rules do not fetter the discretion of the court...[5]

This means that, whereas there might be delay if such applications are submitted later than four months after the date of the proceeding in question, the delay may not necessarily be deemed "undue". The question, therefore, is what constitutes "undue delay"?

Order 16 provides no definition of the term. The courts, therefore, determine, on a case by case basis, whether the prevailing circumstances warrant a finding of "undue delay" or not. The determination of this issue, thus, becomes a question of fact that is resolved on the basis of evidence that is filed in the statement and affidavit supporting the application. A survey of the cases on the issue clearly shows that the courts do not consider mere delay in bringing an application or even the expiration of the four-month time limit regarding applications for *certiorari* as a basis for refusing to grant an application. The yardstick for measuring whether the delay is undue or not appears to be based upon the concept of reasonableness. Hence, if, from the evidence available, the delay in bringing the application is unreasonable, then the courts are likely to come to a finding of undue delay and, therefore, refuse to grant the application. However, if there are extenuating circumstances that make the delay in bringing an application either reasonable or inevitable, then the courts are likely to conclude that there has been no undue delay and, consequently, proceed to grant the application.

This judicial approach is illustrated in *NTN Pty Ltd v PTC*,[6] where the applicant applied for leave to apply for an order of *certiorari* to quash the decision of the Board of PTC to grant a television broadcasting licence to Media Niugini Pty Ltd. The licence in question was granted on 19 November 1985, while the application was filed on 16 April 1986. In deciding whether or not there was undue delay in bringing the action,

---

[5] *Id.*, p. 5. See also *Re Nagi Clan* [1995] PNGLR 13; (1991) N1036 where the Court stressed that the 4 months time limit stated in Order 16 is not mandatory. Hence consideration must be given to the cause of the delay and the reasons provided by the applicant.

[6] Above, note 2.

Wilson J, rejecting counsel for the respondent's submission that the delay was not unreasonable, took into account the following matters presented in the affidavit evidence:

> Allowing four months from [the date on which the licence was granted] the application is 11 months late. NTN through Mr Finlay was aware of the grant of licence on that day and was aware that his company had not been heard on the licence.
>
> On 20 November 1985 Mr Finlay was made aware of the letter from Andrew Yauieb. On 26 March 1986 Mr Yauieb made a statutory declaration concerning the letter. At the latest NTN knew of the contents of the letter in March 1986.
>
> NTN brought its concerns to the notice of relevant parties in the first part of 1986 and also made it clear in dealings with Media Niugini that it did not accept the validity of the licences issued.[7]

His Honour then concluded:

> On the evidence before me I am satisfied that there has been undue delay particularly in view of the fact that the relevant period specified by the Rules of Court for an application such as this is four months.[8]

The decision in *NCDIC v Crusoe Pty Ltd*[9] also shows evidence of the application of the concept of reasonableness in determining undue delay. The events in this case were particularly interesting. On 10 March 1983, the applicant applied to the Town Planning Board for a special purpose lease to the land described as Allotment 29 Section 26 (Reke Street) Boroko. Notwithstanding a follow-up letter of 17 April 1985, the Board failed to respond to the application. Thereafter, without legal title to the land, the applicant proceeded to construct a car-park on the land. On 24 November 1988, the respondent's application for a commercial lease over the undeveloped portions of the land was advertised in the *National Gazette*. The applicant, however, was not informed of this until 7 December 1988. On 9 December 1988, the applicant began disputing the re-zoning, and on 5 January 1989, it lodged a fresh application for a special purpose lease over the land. The court proceedings were commenced on 7 February 1989. In this action, the applicant sought to compel the Board to hear its application dated 10 March 1983, and the fresh application lodged on 5 January 1989. In addition, the applicant asked the Court to quash the decision of the Minister for Lands and Physical Planning, which purported

---

[7] *Id.*, p. 75.

[8] *Id.*, p. 76.

[9] [1993] PNGLR 139.

to allow an appeal from the respondent to re-zone the land from special to commercial purposes.

From the chronology of the events of the case, it was quite clear that there was considerable delay in bringing the application. In deciding whether or not there was undue delay, the Court reasoned as follows:

> Crusoe knew that Lot 29 was zoned or regarded as special use, and it may be inferred that Crusoe knew that, after 1985 the NCDIC was building a car-park on part of Lot 29. Indeed, Crusoe proceeded as if Lot 29 was zoned for special purposes. Its initial approach to the Town Planning Board, on which the NCDIC had representation, was rebuffed. The appeal to the Minister against the Town Planning Board decision was made *without notification to the Town Planning Board or the NCDIC which I hold to be an obviously interested party.* Crusoe argued that the *Town Planning Act* did not require it to notify anybody of the appeal. That is true, but the *Town Planning Act* is, as Mr Paine for Crusoe, remarked, perhaps with some over-statement, 'the most poorly drafted piece of legislation on the books'. It has recently been repealed and replaced by the *Physical Planning Act 1989* (No 39 of 1989).
>
> Crusoe relied on an absence of specific statutory direction to notify other interested parties, presumably in the expectation that their ignorance and their consequent inability to make representations to the Minister, could only further the chances of Crusoe obtaining a decision on appeal in its favour. This is unfair conduct.
>
> The NCDIC was only informed that Lot 29 had been re-zoned on 7 December 1988, although Crusoe's application for a commercial lease over the undeveloped portions of Lot 29 was advertised in the *National Gazette* on 24 November 1988. The NCDIC began disputing the re-zoning on 9 December 1988. On 5 January 1989, the NCDIC lodged a fresh application for a special purpose lease over Lot 29, and on 7 February 1989, it commenced proceedings in court.[10]

On the basis of this evidence, the Court came to the conclusion that:

> It appears that once the NCDIC was aware of what was happening to the re-zoning of Lot 29, it took reasonable steps to protect its interests and so the delay should not be considered as 'undue'.[11]

Finally, the decision in *Ex parte Gurupa*[12] also shows that the concept of reasonableness is the basis for determining whether or not there was undue delay. In this case, the applicant brought an application for *certiorari* two years after the decision of the Secretary of the Department of

[10] Id., p. 149.

[11] *Ibid.*

[12] Above, note 4.

Works to dismiss him from the public service. In determining whether or not there had been undue delay, the Court stressed that the fact that the four months "relevant period", which is the time limit for bringing applications involving the order of *certiorari*, had expired did not provide sufficient basis for ruling that there was undue delay. According to the Court,

> Some account must be taken of the difficulty experienced by people in finding legal advice, getting copies of Court depositions and other decisions, becoming aware of the procedure they must adopt. Their remoteness from a court and advice would also be relevant. Each case must be considered on its merits and it must be apparent that the applicant has made some active attempt to seek redress from the court in a timely manner.[13]

After considering the extenuating factors that might make the delay reasonable, the Court, however, refused leave on the grounds that:

> In this case over five months elapsed before he did anything at all to seek advice and further months before he approached a lawyer. There was a further delay in applying that is not explained. I consider this total of two years an undue delay.[14]

How the Courts Determine Substantial Hardship, etc.

The second relevant issue in the application of the principle of delay is whether the granting of the relief sought "would be likely to cause substantial hardship to, or prejudice the rights of, any person or be detrimental to good administration". To determine this issue, the courts examine, from the evidence available, the likelihood of the occurrence of any of these consequences. From the cases decided on the issue, while it is clear that the courts regard the issue as a question of fact, depending upon the evidence that is filed in the supporting statement and affidavit, there appears to be no rule or standard that is generally applicable. Each case is decided on its own merit by sifting through the evidence to find out any relevant facts that have a bearing on the issue.

---

[13] *Id.*, p. 5. See also *Re Nagi Clan*, above, note 5, where the same factors were taken into consideration in determining undue delay.

[14] *Ibid.* This decision was upheld and followed in *Re Evangelical Lutheran Church of PNG* [1995] PNGLR 276; (1995) N1317.

In *NTN Pty Ltd v PTC*,[15] to determine whether or not granting the relief sought would be likely to cause substantial hardship to Media Niugini (an interested party in the application for leave), the Court took into account that:

> I have received extensive evidence from Media Niugini regarding its commercial commitments to the commencement of broadcast television. While part of its operations have [*sic*] been directed to market television which primarily involved in-house video production and distribution there is no doubt that the Company has made significant capital expenditure to its broadcasting operation. It has amongst other things taken steps to employ and train staff, set up premises, obtain further licences, applied for special leases and constructed a broadcasting tower. It has a co-existing agreement with NTN. It has made capital purchases to equip its production facilities.
>
> NTN claims that many of these expenses could be recouped either through re-sale or by utilizing the equipment through Media Niugini's special relationship with Bond Television in Australia. Even if I were to give some credence to that claim, I am certain that invalidating the licences would have a substantial impact on its commercial viability against the steps it has taken since November 1985 to gear itself towards introducing a broadcasting service.
>
> Media Niugini intends to shortly commence pilot broadcasting with a planned commencement of full broadcasting in August this year. It had its licences renewed since their first issue in November 1985.[16]

The Court concluded on the basis of this evidence that:

> On all of the material before me I am of the clear opinion that granting of the relief sought would be likely to cause substantial hardship to Media Niugini.[17]

Having found, on the basis of the evidence available, that granting the relief sought would be likely to cause substantial hardship to Media Niugini, although there appeared to be insufficient evidence to consider the question of whether or not granting the relief sought would also be detrimental to good administration, the Court nonetheless proceeded to make a finding on the question. It did this by inductively reasoning that:

> ...There comes a time when things are entitled to be as they appear. An applicant who is involved in challenging a decision which has implications for another party or for public administration is under a heavy duty to act expeditiously and fairly.

---

[15] Above, note 2.

[16] *Id.*, p. 76.

[17] *Ibid.*

> The applicant in this case is not entitled to sit on its allegations and claims while to its clear knowledge a party affected continues to make commercial commitments only to seek relief at a time which will be convenient to it.[18]

On the basis of this, it came to the conclusion that, in the circumstances, granting the relief sought would be detrimental to good administration.

From the strained argument that the Court used to support this finding, it appears as if the Court felt compelled to deal with the question even though, as it admitted, "there was no substantial argument on the point". This raises the question as to whether, from the wording of Order 16 Rule 4(1), it is mandatory or necessary at all to do so. The relevant provision of the sub-rule states that:

> ...if, in the opinion of the Court, the granting of the relief sought would be likely to cause substantial hardship to, or prejudice the rights of, any person or would be detrimental to good administration.

This provision refers to three different situations: the first one is where granting the relief sought would be likely to cause substantial hardship to any person; the second one is where granting the relief sought would be likely to cause substantial prejudice to the rights of any person; and the final one is where granting the relief sought would be detrimental to good administration.

The particular way in which this provision is phrased seems to indicate that the intention of the sub-rule is to provide a range of alternative consequences of the decision to grant the relief sought as the basis of the Court's discretion to grant or refuse the relief sought. This leaves the Court free to choose from any of them. For this reason, the three consequences are joined by the word "or" rather than "and", suggesting that each of them is an alternative to the other. Hence, once there is a finding that any one of them is likely to occur, it is sufficient basis for refusing to grant the application for leave or the relief sought. It is, therefore, not necessary to consider the likelihood of the occurrence of the other consequences. Support for this interpretation of the sub-rule may be found in the decision of Brunton J in *NCDIC v Crusoe Pty Ltd*,[19] which was based upon only the situation of whether granting the application would be likely to prejudice the rights of any person, without any mention of the other situations.

---

[18] *Ibid*.

[19] Above, note 9.

CHAPTER 9

AN ARGUABLE CASE

The decision of Wilson J in *NTN Pty Ltd v PTC*[1] suggests that criteria other than those prescribed by Order 16 of the *National Court Rules* (Ch 38) may also be relevant to the decision on leave. In that case, His Honour stated that:

> Applications for leave for judicial review involve the exercise of discretion. Such discretion must be exercised judicially. Once a court is satisfied that the applicant has sufficient interest (O 16, r 3(5)) it then exercises its discretion as to whether leave should be granted. This discretion is embodied in O 16, r 3(1).
>
> In exercising its discretion the court must consider whether the applicant has an arguable case. In *Inland Revenue Commissioners v National Federation of Self-Employed and Small Businesses Ltd* [1982] AC 617, Lord Diplock set out the principles upon which the court should act and I respectfully adopt them. Lord Diplock said at 644:
>
>> 'If, on a quick perusal of the material then available, the court ... thinks that it discloses what might on further consideration turn out to be *an arguable case in favour of granting to the applicant the relief claimed, it ought, in the exercise of a judicial discretion, to give him leave to apply for judicial relief.* The discretion that the court is exercising at this stage is not the same as that which it is called upon to exercise when all the evidence is in and the matter has been fully argued at the hearing of the application.'[2]

This *dicta* has been referred to in numerous cases as authority to support the view that "an arguable case" is also a relevant principle to be applied in the decision on leave. In *Manjin v PTC*,[3] Hinchliffe J referred to the *dicta* credited to Lord Diplock above and, in accordance with it, stated that, "As soon as his Honour is satisfied that the applicant has a sufficient interest and that there is an arguable case then he will more

---

[1] [1987] PNGLR 70.
[2] *Id.*, p. 74.
[3] [1990] PNGLR 288.

than likely grant leave".[4] Sheehan J, relying on the same authority, stated in *Diro v Ombudsman Commission*[5] that:

> The requirement for leave is to enable the courts to sift out at an early stage, applications which are trivial, vexatious or hopeless. This is to ensure that an applicant is only permitted to proceed to a substantive hearing inter partes if the Court can be satisfied there is an arguable case for review. *Inland Revenue Commissioners v National Federation of Self-Employed and Small Businesses Ltd* [1981] 2 WLR 722.[6]

In the recent case of *Geno v PNG,*[7] the Supreme Court endorsed the relevance of "an arguable case" in deciding on leave. The Court referred to the above *dicta* of Wilson J and stated categorically that, "The principles applicable to an application for leave are now well settled [in] *NTN Pty Ltd v PTC*".[8]

How the Courts Determine an Arguable Case

The principle of an arguable case is essentially a *prima facie* view that is formed by the court after "a quick perusal" of the evidence before it. This view is usually based upon an assumption or a provisional finding that an application raises substantive legal issues that require a judicial determination, and the applicant has a sufficient interest in the matter to request adjudication of the issues. The determination of an arguable case is a question of fact and degree, depending on the evidence available to the court, as to the existence or otherwise of a case that merits examination by the court.

In *NTN Pty Ltd v PTC*, the applicant sought leave to apply for judicial review of the decision of the Board of PTC granting broadcasting licences to Media Niugini pursuant to section 6 of the *Radiocommunications Act* (Ch 152). On the authority of Lord Diplock's *dicta* that an arguable case is a relevant criterion for determining whether to grant or refuse leave, Wilson J observed that:

---

[4] *Id.*, p. 290.
[5] [1991] PNGLR 153.
[6] *Id.*, p. 154.
[7] [1993] PNGLR 22.
[8] *Id.*, p. 23.

> The submission advanced by Mr Molloy [Counsel for the applicant] would no doubt, if successfully argued, involve some development of the principles of natural justice and administrative law... I mention this section as it is a matter which in my view should form part of a court's consideration in exercising its discretion on whether or not to grant leave where it has some hesitation, as I do in this case, as to whether the applicant has an arguable case.[9]

Potential Arguability

The point worth noting here is that leave in this case was granted not because the applicant's case had any merit. On the contrary, the basis for granting leave was simply that there was evidence, indicated by counsel for applicant's submission, that the application had "what might on further consideration turn out to be an arguable case". This approach of applying the principle of an arguable case requires that once fundamental, serious or genuine issues of law (e.g. constitutional or statutory interpretation, application of legal principles or doctrines, etc.) are raised, which issues merit judicial determination, then regardless of the merit of the case, an applicant should be granted leave. It is, therefore, referred to as the "potential arguability" approach.

Several decisions of the National Court reflect this approach of applying the principle. One example is the decision in *Arawe Logging Pty Ltd v PNG.*[10] In handing down judgment in this case, Brunton AJ emphasised the point that his reason for granting leave to the applicant was based not upon the merit of the case but on the fact that the applicant had a sufficient interest and because:

> The issues of law that are raised by this case are in my view *genuine issues of law that raise serious questions.* It is not for me to decide those questions one way or another, merely, to say that they are bona fide issues that could be tried.[11]

The reasoning of Woods J in *Amadio Pty Ltd v PNG*[12] also follows the "potential arguability" approach. In that case, the applicant applied for leave to apply for judicial review of the decision of the Minister for

---

[9] Above, note 1 at 74.

[10] [1988-89] PNGLR 216.

[11] *Id.*, p. 217. (Emphasis added.)

[12] [1992] PNGLR 218.

Minerals and Energy which purported to extend the Petroleum Prospecting Authority of the fourth defendant. Having determined that the applicant had a sufficient interest, Woods J proceeded to consider whether the applicant had an arguable case or not. After a quick perusal of the evidence available to the court, he stated quite significantly that:

> I will not go here into the details deposed to support the above submission, but there was enough material to enable me to consider that *there may be an arguable case* for the plaintiff to have the decision-making process reviewed."[13]

Another case that follows the potential arguability approach is *Geno v PNG.*[14] This was an appeal against a National Court decision refusing leave. Amet J (as he then was), who decided the case in the trial court, gave the following elaborate reasons for refusing to grant the application for leave. According to him:

> The defendant has, whilst conceding that the Plaintiffs have sufficient interest and an arguable case, posed what, in my opinion, is a fundamental policy issue as to whether or not it is appropriate to grant leave in an application such as this, involving as it does a service of the defendant.
>
> Is it appropriate that a service of the defendant should be granted leave to challenge an administrative decision of the defendant which might have little practical benefit which dispute could not be resolved administratively? Is it going to serve any practical purpose to pursue this application, or might it cause unnecessary administrative inconvenience which could adequately be addressed administratively? What is to be the balance of convenience at the end of the day, even though, as the defendant conceded, the defendant failed to consult the plaintiffs? What is to be the practical efficacy of granting the declarations sought?
>
> I hold the view that, as a matter of practical politics and administrative efficiency, effectiveness and convenience, inter-governmental agency, departments or services should be discouraged from resorting to litigation to resolve what can, in most instances, be amicably and more effectively resolved to total benefit of the State. What this requires, in my view, is a greater effort at establishing and developing constructive and meaningful dialogue and consultation instead of the adversarial litigious position so readily resorted to.
>
> I consider it most inappropriate that departments or agencies of the State services should have to resort to litigation to resolve

---

[13] *Id.*, p. 221. (Emphasis added.)

[14] Above, note 7.

> administrative differences of opinion which could be amicably resolved to the satisfaction of all parties with a little more dialogue and consultation. Extreme legal positions need not be taken if, by some practical concessions, a practical resolution of the difference or dispute is arrived at for the mutual benefit of both parties concerned.
> Even more inappropriate, in my view, is that a State service. department, agency or institution should have to resort to litigation against the parent State, such as in this case. If the error or irregularity can be identified, acknowledged and rectified without need to resort to litigation, then that alternate dispute resolution process should be encouraged and litigation discouraged.[15]

The Supreme Court rejected all these reasons as irrelevant. It ruled that the question as to whether granting the declaration sought would serve "any practical purpose", "practical efficacy", "balance of convenience" or "cause unnecessary administrative inconvenience" is a matter to be considered at the substantive stage of the application for judicial review and not relevant at the leave stage. The Supreme Court, therefore, reversed the National Court decision, and held that:

> ... [T]he trial judge erred in law when he stated in the same passage that it was a matter of fundamental policy issue as to whether the appellants should be granted leave as a service of the defendant. With respect, it is not a question of policy. *The issue is whether there is a cause of action in law* and whether the appellants have any sufficient interest in the matter...
> ... The desirability of the court to settle a matter out of court without the willingness of the parties is no valid ground for refusing to exercise discretion in favour of granting leave for judicial review. The trial judge fell into error in this regard.
> We should also point out that the issue in this case is not simply one of an administrative matter. *The issue is one of non-compliance with s 193(3) of the Constitution and the consequences that flow from such non-compliance.*[16]

[15] *Id.*, pp. 25, 26.

[16] *Id.*, pp. 26, 27. (Emphasis added.) The Supreme Court also held, as an error of law, that "once the respondent conceded the above matters [i.e. that the applicant had a sufficient interest and there was an arguable case], the trial judge should have exercised his discretion in favour of granting leave for judicial review". The effect of this holding would seem to transfer the responsibility for making the decision on leave from the judge to the defendant (respondent). Rule 3(5) of Order 16 specifically refers to the Court, and no one else, as the decision- maker in applications for leave. It says in the clearest terms that "*The Court shall not grant leave unless it considers* that the applicant has a sufficient interest in the matter to which the application relates." The decision to grant or refuse leave has always been, and remains so under the law, an exclusive judicial right and privilege which has to be exercised at the discretion of the judge. The

From the Supreme Court's decision, it appears that the Court considered the non-compliance with section 193(3) of the *Constitution* and the consequences that flow from such non-compliance as evidence that there was an arguable case. The fact that merely having a cause of action in law, without any regard to the merits of the case, was held to meet the requirements of the principle of an arguable case shows that the Supreme Court endorsed the potential arguability approach of applying the principle of an arguable case.

Actual Arguability

There are indications, however, that the practice of applying the principle of an arguable case is not always consistent. While some judges consider the potential arguability of the case enough to meet the requirements of the principle, other judges appear to insist on the "actual", rather than the potential, arguability of the case. This method of applying the principle is referred to as the actual arguability approach. This approach requires that the merits of the case in an application for leave be examined, even if cursorily, at the leave stage in order to form a *prima facie* view of the case. The *prima facie* view thus formed is based upon a "reasonable suspicion" that there are valid grounds for applying for judicial review and, for that matter, the applicant has a sufficient interest to apply to the court to have the matter reviewed.[17]

There are many decisions which adopt this approach. One example is the decision of Amet J (as he then was) in *Sigulogo v Leadership Tribunal*.[18] In that case, the applicant applied for leave to apply for judicial review of several decisions and recommendations of a Leadership Tribunal. In considering whether to grant leave or not, Amet J, without reference to any relevant authority on the issue, held that:

---

defendant's view on the matter before the court or, as in this case, the defendant's concession that the applicant had a sufficient interest and an arguable case, cannot, and should not, be permitted to modify or abridge the rule of court. The respondent's view of how the decision should be made cannot, therefore, be substituted for the view of the judge. Otherwise, that would be tantamount to an abuse of process.

[17] *Inland Revenue Commissioners v National Federation of Self-Employed and Small Businesses Ltd* [1981] 2 All ER 93 at 106; [1982] AC 617 at 643; [1981] 2 WLR 722 at 739.

[18] (1990) N829.

> ... *[T]he arguments as to the merits of the case to be argued,* in relation to grounds alleging errors of law and severity of the penalties, *I do not consider have any merit.* There being no other ground for granting leave I refuse leave for judicial review.[19]

The key element in this judgment that indicates the way in which the principle of an arguable case was applied is the fact that the application for leave was decided on the merits of the case after an examination of the substantive grounds supporting the application. The puzzling aspect of the judgment is that it was made by the same judge who laid down the rule in *Ombudsman Commission v Donohoe*[20] that the Court is not required to address the substantive legal issues raised in an application for leave at the leave stage. Why His Honour chose to deviate from a rule established by himself on this occasion is not clear.

Another case that followed the actual arguability approach is *Vanderlist v Mount Hagen Golf Club.*[21] This was an application for leave to apply for judicial review of the decision of the Mount Hagen Golf Club which purported to suspend the membership of the applicant for 12 months. In determining whether to grant leave or not, Woods J examined the substantive grounds of the application (in this instance, the issue of natural justice) and ruled that:

> In the circumstances I can see no grounds at all for the Court to be able to apply its own discretion to the matter of the suspension of a member of a voluntary organisation once a breach of the rules has been committed and a fair hearing has taken place into the matter. All members have bound themselves voluntarily to certain rules and have agreed that if they breach these rules they risk suspension. *I am not going to interfere in that procedure once I have been satisfied that the member has been given a fair hearing.* I cannot impose my own discretion onto a club as to whether 3 months, 6 months, 9 months or 12 months suspension is appropriate where there is no question of livelihood involved.
>
> In the circumstances therefore I feel that leave should be refused.[22]

It should be noted that Woods J's decision in *Amadio Pty Ltd v PNG*, as indicated above, followed the potential arguability approach. That case, incidentally, was decided subsequent to this one.

---

[19] *Id.*, p. 5.
[20] Ref. [1985] PNGLR 348.
[21] [1990] PNGLR 315.
[22] *Id.*, p. 316.

In *Application of Gigimat*,[23] Woods J again followed the actual arguability approach. In that case, the applicant applied for leave to seek judicial review of the decisions of certain officers of the Post and Telecommunications Corporation to suspend and dismiss the applicant from the employment of the Corporation. In deciding whether to grant or refuse leave, His Honour briefly perused the facts of the case and stated that:

> The established principles in seeking leave for judicial review emphasise that an applicant must show that he has an arguable case. The court in considering leave to review is not necessarily concerned with the merits of the decision in respect of which the review is sought but rather the decision-making process itself...
>
> So, does the applicant have an arguable case here? Has there been an error in the decision making process?[24]

To answer this question, His Honour examined the evidence against the background of the established grounds on which administrative decisions of this nature can be reviewed. He then concluded that:

> The evidence before me is that the applicant was a senior officer of the Corporation with a responsibility which included the accounting and security of cash received in the office of the Corporation for which he was responsible. Any employer or corporation is entitled to expect a high standard of responsibility where money is involved. The Corporation had found a serious discrepancy and was entitled to call the applicant to account. The Corporation followed the correct procedures for dealing with an employee in such a situation. It gave him a chance to put his case or explanation. When the officer of the Corporation was not satisfied with the explanation, it made a decision it was empowered to do. Moreover, that officer then drew the applicant's attention to the appropriate review procedure, which the applicant then availed himself of, to no avail. *I can find no errors in the decision-making process. The Corporation was quite entitled to terminate for such a breach of responsibility involving money, and the procedures for a fair hearing were followed.*[25]

As the conclusion indicates, His Honour refused to grant leave because the application lacked merit.[26]

---

[23] [1992] PNGLR 322.

[24] *Id.*, pp. 323-324.

[25] Id., p. 324. (Emphasis added.)

[26] See also *Ex parte Gurupa* (1990) N856, where Doherty AJ indicated that it was necessary for the applicant to show by evidence that the Secretary of the Department of Works had committed an error of law in order to be granted leave.

Finally, the decision in *Application of Kandau*[27] also followed the actual arguability approach. This case was brought seeking leave to review the decision of the Corrective Institution Service Appeal Board to demote the applicant from a sergeant to a lance corporal. In determining whether the applicant had an arguable case or not, Woods J, again, examined the evidence before the Court, weighed it against the established grounds of judicial review, and held, based upon the merits, that:

> Whilst this is only an application for leave for review, it is quite clear to me on the bare history of the matter that the applicant has been dealt with in accordance with the regulations that apply to the Correctional Service...
> *I find that the appropriate procedures were followed* and this application seems to be more in the vein of an appeal against a harsh and oppressive punishment. *I must be satisfied that there may have been a miscarriage of justice in the internal operation of the Correctional Institutions Service before I can grant leave for review.* It is not the role of the court to interfere too readily with the disciplinary punishments given in a disciplined force.
> I refuse leave for judicial review.[28]

The Quest for a Better Approach

The actual arguability approach to determining whether there is an arguable case or not is riddled with logical as well as legal problems. As indicated above, the approach inevitably requires an assessment of the merits of the case. Yet, a fair ruling on the merits of case, as Amet J rightly points out, requires "an assessment of all the evidence and the benefit of legal arguments".[29] On account of the summary nature of the *ex parte* proceedings, the courts are not presented with extensive evidence, nor are they permitted to hear legal arguments. In practice, applicants for leave, as a rule, do not usually present all their evidence at the leave stage, nor are they bound to do so.[30] Even if they did, sometimes a "quick perusal" of the

---

[27] [1992] PNGLR 300.
[28] *Id.*, p. 302. (Emphasis added.) See also *Application of Posai* [1995] PNGLR 350; (1995) N 1354, which followed the same approach.
[29] Above, note 20 at 361.
[30] Above, note 3.

material may not be adequate to make a ruling on the merits of the case. On account of this, a determination of an arguable case which adopts the actual arguability approach, rather than the potential arguability approach, is a premature assessment of the merits of the case and is likely to prejudice the applicant's case.

Furthermore, the actual arguability approach seems to confuse the arguability of a case with the probability of the success or failure of the case. While the potential arguability approach is concerned with the presence or absence of genuine legal issues that require a judicial determination, the actual arguability approach involves an assessment of the relative merits of the case and a decision on the probability of the success or failure of the substantive trial.

Without the aid of scientific techniques, a decision on the probability of the success or failure of the substantive trial at the leave stage is highly susceptible to the fallacy that an application for judicial review which, on the face, lacks merit (either because of incomplete evidence or the incompetence of, or unprofessional presentation by, counsel) is certain to fail. To illustrate the fallacy of this reasoning, let us assume, *arguendo*, that a judge, using the actual arguability approach to determine the arguability of a case, rules that an applicant has no arguable case. What does this mean in terms of probability?

First, it could mean the probability of the case being unsuccessful at the hearing stage, based upon evidence from the statement and the affidavit supporting. This assessment, of course, is premature in the sense that the decision is being made before an assessment of all the evidence and the benefit of legal arguments. Secondly, the ruling could also mean the probability of the unsuccessful outcome of the substantive trial, if no further evidence is adduced to support the application for judicial review. In other words, as well as ruling on the outcome of the trial, the judge is also ruling on the unlikelihood of the applicant's ability to discover further evidence that might change the outcome of the case at the substantive stage of the trial. Yet the applicant may be able to present new evidence at the hearing stage which could modify the odds, providing a chance of success. Even though this may not guarantee a successful outcome, it reduces the probability of an unsuccessful outcome of the substantive trial, and at the same time, casts doubt on any decision on the probability of the success or failure of the substantive trial that is made at the leave stage. This shows that the actual arguability approach to determining the existence of an arguable case (which is based upon the relative merits of the case) runs quite a high risk of resulting in a miscarriage of justice[31] and makes a clear case for judges to adopt the potential arguability approach.

[31] The risk of miscarriage of justice that can result from such a fallacy was highlighted in a recent important English Court of Appeal case (R v Deen) in which the Bayesian inference theory was applied to secure a retrial of a convicted rapist. For a commentary on this case, see R Mathews "Improving the Odds on Justice?", *New Scientist*, 16 April 1994, pp. 12-13.

CHAPTER 10

EXHAUSTION OF ADMINISTRATIVE REMEDIES

The final legal principle that is considered relevant to the decision on leave is the exhaustion of administrative remedies. This criterion, like the one relating to an arguable case, is not provided for in Order 16. It is adopted from the common law doctrine of exhaustion.[1] Designed to ensure that the judicial review process is used only as a last resort to resolve legal issues, the principle requires that, as a condition for granting leave, an applicant should make a genuine effort to have the matter resolved through available alternative methods of challenge, such as statutory right of appeal to an administrative authority. These alternative remedies normally consist of channels of appeal to a hierarchy of persons or bodies within the governmental organization through which decisions made by subordinate persons or bodies within the organization are reviewed.

For example, a decision made by the departmental secretary of a particular ministry may be appealed to the minister responsible for that ministry. If the appeal is successful, it would save the aggrieved person the cost of going to court as well as saving the court's time. On the other hand, if the appeal is unsuccessful, recourse to the courts may be permitted. It should be pointed out that if the procedure for obtaining an alternative remedy is expensive or otherwise damaging to a person, the courts may waive the requirement of exhaustion. Otherwise, the courts will invariably insist, as the Supreme Court did in *PNG v Kapal*,[2] that "this threshold question be decided before the National Court invokes its judicial review jurisdiction".[3]

---

[1] See *De Smith's Judicial Review of Administrative Action* (4th edn) by J M Evans (ed) (London: Sweet & Maxwell 1980).

[2] [1987] PNGLR 417.

[3] *Id.*, p. 422.

How the Courts Determine Exhaustion

The first reported case that applied the doctrine of exhaustion is *PNG v Kapal.*[4] This was an appeal against the decision of the National Court which declared that the suspension of the Western Highlands Provincial Government by the National Executive Council (NEC) was void and of no effect. During the appeal, it was pointed out that section 187E(1) of the *Constitution* provides that the NEC only has power to provisionally suspend a provincial government, and that such suspension is subject to confirmation by Parliament. The procedures for confirmation or otherwise were set out in the now-repealed *Organic Law on Provincial Government.* Since the NEC decision had not been confirmed by Parliament, the Supreme Court considered it an error on the part of the trial judge for failing to take into account the fact the procedures set out in the *Organic Law on Provincial Government* for confirmation had not been completed. Accordingly, it held that proceedings for judicial review of a decision of the National Executive Council to provisionally suspend a provincial government should not be entertained where the procedures provided for in the *Organic Law on Provincial Government* have not been completed or exhausted.

On the belief that this matter raised an issue of exhaustion of administrative remedies, Kidu CJ and Woods J, after chastising the trial judge for failing to address the issue, explained the principle as follows:

> One of the fundamental rules in relation to judicial review is the question as to whether the applicant for judicial review has exhausted other remedies provided by law, eg, statutory provisions for appeal. Generally, it is the rule that the judicial review jurisdiction will not be exercised where other remedies available have not been used. See, eg, *R v Epping & Harlow General Commissioners; Ex parte Goldstraw* [1983] 3 All ER 257 at p. 262 per Sir John Donaldson MR (with Purchas LJ concurring). This rule is subject to cases where facts and circumstances show that judicial review is more appropriate or convenient to do justice.[5]

Although this *dicta* accurately expresses the rule regarding the principle of exhaustion of administrative remedies, its application in the particular circumstances of this case seems rather mistaken. In the first

---

[4] Above, note 2.

[5] *Id.*, p. 421.

place, the principle deals essentially with administrative remedies. Such remedies consist of extra-judicial remedial action (often referred to as alternative remedies) which are taken by a higher public official or body in the process of reviewing the decision of a subordinate public official or body that is brought before it on appeal. Clearly, whether the NEC decision had been confirmed by Parliament or not has no connection whatsoever with administrative remedies, because the confirmation is not triggered by an appeal.

Secondly, the principle places the burden of exhausting the available administrative remedies on the applicant for judicial review and not on the respondent whose decision is being challenged. As the Supreme Court rightly stated, the question is "whether *the applicant for judicial review* has exhausted other remedies provided by law". Hence, assuming *arguendo* that the Supreme Court justices were right in considering exhaustion as a relevant issue in this case, since the State was the respondent in the application for leave, it would not have been necessary, let alone meaningful, for the trial court to take exhaustion into consideration.

Judging from the circumstances of the case, the question which was most apposite was whether the NEC decision, in view of the fact that it was only provisional, may be challenged in court before it was confirmed by Parliament. In other words, was the decision of the NEC a final decision? The relevant principles applicable here are those derived from the doctrine of ripeness, which has been popularised by the American courts. This doctrine requires that in order for a case to be "ripe" for judicial determination or consideration, it must involve issues which are real, present or imminent and not those which are abstract, hypothetical or remote.[6] Under this doctrine, if an applicant seeks leave to challenge the validity of a decision which is neither final nor self-executory, the fact that the decision is subject to changing circumstances and no attempt is made to enforce it will result in the refusal of the application on the ground that the case is not "ripe" for judicial determination. On the other hand, if a public body makes a decision and threatens to enforce it against

[6] See *Columbia Broadcasting System v United States* (1942) 316 US 407; 62 S Ct 1194. The doctrine, otherwise known as "Justice Harlan's Calculus" was carefully formulated and refined by Justice Harlan in *Abbott Laboratories v Gardner* (1967) 387 US 136.

some persons or a particular defaulter, then, although the decision is not final, the threat of punishment would constitute a valid reason for granting leave to challenge the legal validity of the decision. The validity of such a decision may then be challenged at the substantive stage of the trial on the ground of procedural *ultra vires*, which deals with the question of the legal validity of a decision which is made in breach of laid down procedure.

Notwithstanding the misapplication of the principle, the rules of the principle of exhaustion of administrative remedies stated in *PNG v Kapal* have been adopted and applied in subsequent cases. In *Kekedo v Burns Philp (PNG) Ltd,*[7] the Supreme Court endorsed the rules and elaborated on them. This was an appeal against the National Court's decision to grant leave to the respondents to apply for judicial review of a decision of the appellant as Secretary for the Department of Labour and Employment. The principal ground of the appeal was that the respondents had not exhausted the available statutory remedy of appeal to the Minister under section 9(4) of the *Employment of Non-Citizens Act* (Ch 374) before invoking the judicial review power of the National Court. From the facts of the case, it was clear that the respondents were aware of the availability of the statutory right of appeal to the Minister. Indeed, they actually did lodge an appeal to the Minister, but did so five days after having obtained leave from the National Court to apply for judicial review. According to counsel for the respondents, this course of action was taken in order to save the respondents' option to pursue the alternative remedy should the application for judicial review be unsuccessful.

The question then arose as to whether the existence of an alternative statutory remedy can oust the judicial review jurisdiction of the National Court. In other words, did the fact that the respondent had a statutory right of appeal to the Minister take away his right to apply to the Court if he chose to bypass the appeal to the Minister and apply to the Court in the first instance? In answering this question, Amet J (as he then was), in a concurring judgment, agreed with counsel for respondents' argument that the existence of an alternative remedy does not oust the inherent supervisory review jurisdiction of the Court. It, thus, did not affect the right to apply to the Court in the first instance. As he put it, "the equitable

---

[7] [1988-89] PNGLR 122.

and, indeed, inherent constitutional supervisory review jurisdiction of the National and Supreme Courts cannot be ousted altogether by provision of statutory administrative alternate (*sic*) remedies."[8]

Counsel for the respondents also submitted that the existence of an alternative remedy could not take away the respondents' right to apply to the Court, because the statutory right of appeal to the Minister did not provide for a full inquiry or a stay of enforcement of the decision appealed against. This meant that, in the particular circumstance of the case, the appeal to the Minister could not be properly regarded as an alternative remedy, more so since it was not dispositive. On the basis of this argument, counsel concluded that the mere existence of an alternative statutory remedy was irrelevant to the issue of exhaustion and should, therefore, not be accepted as a valid ground of appeal. In the alternative, he argued that even if the existence of an alternative remedy was relevant in the circumstances, then since the decision to grant leave is a discretionary one and the available administrative remedy was not dispositive, the National Court's decision should be read as a discretionary one which had considered the issue of exhaustion but declined to regard the appeal to the Minister as an alternative remedy because it was not dispositive.

Amet J, however, flatly rejected these arguments. He pointed out, correctly, that the adequacy of the available alternative administrative remedy or the fact that the available alternative remedy was not dispositive did not permit the respondent to dispense with it. This was especially so since, in the particular circumstances of the case, it would have resulted in an abuse of process if the respondent were allowed to first exhaust judicial remedies and then revert to explore the alternative administrative remedy. In his words:

> Parliament has, on the basis of the public policy considerations that I have alluded to, which can be inferred, deliberately enacted a statutory administrative remedial option which, although it is not exclusive and does not necessarily oust the supervisory constitutional jurisdiction of the superior courts, as a general rule, should be exhausted before recourse is had to the courts.
>
> I do not consider that any exceptional circumstances exist in this case not to adhere to the general rule...[9]

---

[8] *Id.*, p. 126.

[9] *Id.*, p. 127.

The Supreme Court, therefore, allowed the appeal and quashed the order granting leave on the basis of the following common law principles:

> Save in the most exceptional circumstances, the rule is that judicial review jurisdiction will not be exercised by the Court where other remedies are available.
>
> Whether the statutory procedure would be quicker, or slower than procedure by way of judicial review; whether the matter depends on some particular or technical knowledge which is more readily available to the alternative appellant body are amongst the matters which a court may take into account when considering the exercise of discretion. The fact that judicial review is quicker and convenient is of itself not sufficient ground for the exercise of jurisdiction.[10]

In applying these principles, the Court reasoned that the respondents had failed to bring themselves within the exceptions to the rule. Since an appeal to the Minister was pending, it then ordered that this appeal should be allowed to proceed. It may be observed that this decision to allow the appeal to Minister to proceed and be exhausted before the respondent be permitted to invoke the judicial review jurisdiction of the National Court was not only the most reasonable thing to do under the circumstances. It was also consistent with the objective of the principle of exhaustion of administrative remedies.

The Supreme Court decision above was followed in *Central Pomio Logging Corpn Pty Ltd v PNG.*[11] This was a case in which the Collector of Customs at Rabaul refused to grant the plaintiff clearance of his ship and its cargo of logs. The basis of the refusal was that there was a group of logs among the logs loaded on the ship which were referred to as "fresh logs". These logs were allegedly loaded without being checked by the forestry officers for species identification, scaling and grading. Under section 178 of the *Customs Act* (Ch 101),[12] the plaintiff had a right to refer the matter to the Comptroller of Customs in Port Moresby, which he

---

[10] *Id.*, p. 124. The principles were extracted from *R v Chief Constable; Ex parte Calveley* [1986] 1 QB 424; [1986] 1 All ER 257; [1986] 2 WLR 144.

[11] [1990] PNGLR 195.

[12] Section 178 of the *Customs Act* (Ch 101) provides that: "(1) If a dispute as to a matter of not involving a contravention of this Act arises under this Act or in relation to the customs, the matter may, at the request of the persons interested, be referred to the Comptroller for decision and the Comptroller may, in such manner as he thinks proper, inform himself as to the circumstances, and determine the matter."

did. Subsequently, the plaintiff brought this judicial review action seeking, among other things, an order of *mandamus* to compel the customs officer to consider his application for clearance. The issue was whether the plaintiff, having exercised the option or right to refer the matter to the Comptroller of Customs, can now by way of judicial review deal with the same matter?

Relying on the authority of the Supreme Court decision in *Kekedo v Burns Philp (PNG) Ltd*, the Court held that:

> Where a person wishes to challenge a decision of the Collector of Customs under the *Customs Act*, he has an option of whether to proceed by way of judicial review under O 16 of the *National Court Rules* or to proceed by way of the review provisions set out under the *Customs Act*. Whether or not he may proceed by way of judicial review is in the discretion of the National Court and the principles for exercising this discretion are set out in *Kekedo v Burns Philp (PNG) Ltd*. If the person chooses to do this, then he may, of course, appeal all the way up to the Supreme Court. If however, a party decides not to proceed by way of judicial review but by way of the procedure laid out under the *Customs Act*, in my view, this is an election and he cannot pursue the matter by way of judicial review. Such a person may apply by way of judicial review of the decision of the Comptroller...The plaintiff has not sought the judicial review of the decision of the Comptroller of Customs...[13]

This *dicta*, in its entirety, correctly expresses the principle of exhaustion. One may add, by way of clarification, that notwithstanding whichever option a person elects to challenge a decision under the *Customs Act*, the principle of exhaustion will inevitably have to be taken into account. This is because, even where an aggrieved person elects not to proceed by way of judicial review but by way of the procedure laid out under the *Customs Act*, since "the equitable and, indeed, inherent constitutional supervisory review jurisdiction of the National and Supreme Courts cannot be ousted altogether by provision of statutory administrative alternate remedies",[14] the person may, after appealing to the Comptroller of Customs, seek judicial review of the decision of the Comptroller. As the Court rightly pointed out, if the plaintiff had sought the judicial review of the decision of the Comptroller of Customs and not that of the Collector of Customs, as counsel for the applicant erroneously did, the Court would have been favourably disposed to considering the application. This is

[13] Above, note 11 at 199.
[14] Above, note 7 at 126.

because, since the Comptroller of Customs is the highest decision-making official under the Act, an appeal to him would have exhausted the available alternative administrative remedies.

PART IV

THE DECISION ON LEAVE

CHAPTER 11

THE LEAVE DECISION - MAKING PROCESS

Grounds Upon Which Leave May Be Granted or Refused

The discussion of the matters relevant to the exercise of the court's discretion in granting or refusing leave shows that the decision on leave is supposed to be based upon a set of four different legal principles. These are:

1. *Locus standi*
2. Undue delay
3. An arguable case, and
4. Exhaustion of administrative remedies.

A review of the decisions on leave, however, shows that judges apply these principles rather selectively, with little or no regard to consistency, uniformity or regularity. In the majority of cases, the only principle that was considered in the determination of leave applications is the sufficient interest of the applicant.[1] A few cases considered only the principle of an arguable case, to the exclusion of all other principles.[2] On rare occasions, some cases considered the sufficient interest of the applicant together with the principle of an arguable case. Where these two principles were considered together, it was invariably required that the conditions of both principles must be met before leave may be granted.[3] The principle of undue delay was rarely considered unless it was raised by the respondent (where intervention was permitted) during the leave application or on appeal. Where it was considered independently by the judge, it was sometimes combined with the principle of an arguable case[4] or *locus standi*. Similarly, the principle of exhaustion was considered only during

[1] In one exceptional case, a decision on leave was made without any reference whatsoever to the sufficient interest of the applicant. See *Application of Gigimat* [1992] PNGLR 322.
[2] *Ibid.* and *Application of Kandau* [1992] PNGLR 300.
[3] See *NTN Pty Ltd v PTC* [1987] PNGLR 70; *Manjin v PTC* [1990] PNGLR 288; *Geno v PNG* [1993] PNGLR 22; and *Diro v Ombudsman Commission* [1991] PNGLR 153.
[4] See *Ex parte Gurupa* (1990) N856.

the substantive trial[5] or on appeal,[6] rather than during leave applications.

These variations in the application of the relevant legal principles raise fundamental questions about the grounds upon which leave may be granted or refused. Are judges required to apply all the principles that are relevant to the exercise of the court's discretion in every case? If so, in what order? Otherwise, how are they supposed to determine which principle is to be applied in different cases? In other words, what circumstances give rise to the applicability of the various principles? Do all of them carry equal weight? If not, then what is the relative weight of each principle? Is a decision based upon only a single principle valid? Otherwise, assuming that more than one principle is considered, is it necessary that the requirements of all the principles be met before leave is granted? If not, then which ones are necessary and how many are necessary or sufficient for a valid decision on leave?

Of course, none of these questions have ever been raised in any decided case. This is probably because they border on the matters within the court's discretion and, therefore, tend to be mistakenly regarded as discretionary. Accordingly, individual judges have extended their discretion to grant or refuse leave to the choice of the relevant principles as well. In the process, the choice of the principles is often made on a pragmatic basis. As a result, before a judicial determination is made, the question as to which legal principles will be applied in a particular case is anyone's guess and a legal counsel's nightmare.

The legal principles that are relevant to the exercise of the court's discretion, as explained above, provide a guide or framework for the exercise of the court's discretion. As such, the court's discretion is circumscribed by the parameters of these principles. This means that while judges are free to take into account any factors that, in their opinion, are considered to be relevant to making a decision on leave, they cannot exercise their discretion to by-pass or waive the consideration of a legal principle that is necessary to validate a judgment. Thus, for example, as an exercise of discretion, a judge may determine from the circumstances of the case that an applicant is a busybody and, therefore, has not got sufficient interest in the matter to which the application

---

[5] See *Central Pomio Logging Pty Ltd v PNG* [1990] PNGLR 195.

[6] See *Kekedo v Burns Philp (PNG) Ltd* [1988-89] PNGLR 122.

relates. However, it is not open to the judge, as part of the exercise of discretion, to dispense with the requirement of *locus standi* in deciding on leave.

The leave hurdle plays a fundamental role in regulating the public's access to the courts. It is, therefore, profoundly important that the decision of the National Court to grant or refuse an application for leave to apply for judicial review is made, and be seen to be made, in a fair and just way. Besides, judicial review calls upon the judges to pass judgment on the exercise of discretion by others. This makes it all the more crucial that the decision of the judges itself must be principled and conform to the standards of rational decision-making. In order to meet these standards, the process by which an application for leave is judged must be uniform and systematic, and the choice of the relevant legal principles must be systematic, settled and consistently applied. In the absence of any rules regarding the systematic application of the relevant legal principles, the following proposals are advocated as a guide to the application of the principles.

Proposals for Systematic Decision-Making Process

By law, the first and the most important legal principle that should be considered in the decision on leave is the sufficient interest of the applicant in the matter to which the application relates. This is because it is specifically required by Order 16 as a condition for the grant of leave. As Rule 3(5) expressly states: The Court is enjoined not to grant leave "unless the applicant has a sufficient interest in the matter to which the application relates". These plain words of limitation impose a fetter on the court's discretion to grant leave.

Indeed, the supreme importance of this legal principle to the decision on leave is implicitly acknowledged by the common law principle which regards the sufficient interest of the applicant as a threshold question in all applications for leave. Hence, the sufficient interest of the applicant should not only be the first legal principle to be considered but should be regarded as a necessary condition for a valid decision on leave. This means that it should be mandatory for the courts to consider it in all applications for leave. If the decision on this issue is favourable to the applicant, then, and only then, may the court proceed to consider the other legal principles. However, if the court determines that the applicant lacks sufficient interest in the matter to which the application relates, then there is no need to consider the other legal principles, and leave may be validly refused on this ground alone.

Assuming that the applicant is deemed to have sufficient interest, the next legal principle that should be considered in the decision on leave should be the principle of an arguable case. This is not only logical but is also supported by case authority. Indeed, the context in which the principle was developed clearly indicates that it is not to be considered independently. As an appendage of the sufficient interest principle, it is always considered together with the sufficient interest of the applicant. As Wilson J expressed it,

> Once a court is satisfied that the applicant has sufficient interest (O 16, r 3(5)) it then exercises its discretion as to whether leave should be granted...
>
> In exercising its discretion the court must consider whether the applicant has an arguable case.[7]

Unlike the sufficient interest principle, however, the importance of the principle of an arguable case to the decision on leave should be considered as secondary since there is nothing to indicate that it is mandatory for the courts to consider it in every application for leave. The requirement of an arguable case is a rule of the courts developed by the English courts to save the courts' time. This rule was formulated by Lord Diplock in *Inland Revenue Commissioners v National Federation of Self-Employed and Small Businesses Ltd.*[8] Being a post-independence decision of an English court, it is not binding on the courts in Papua New Guinea. It could also be argued that the requirements of the principle possibly undermine the objective of Order 16, which is that, once an applicant has a sufficient interest in the matter to which the application relates, leave ought to be granted for the application to be heard.

These factors, plus the difficulty that the courts have experienced in applying the principle of an arguable case, raise questions about the justification for retaining it. In fact, there is no evidence that the quality of the decision-making process would in any way be adversely affected

---

[7] *NTN v PTC*, above, note 3 at 74.

[8] [1982] AC 617; [1981] 2 All ER 93; [1981] 2 WLR 722.

by abolishing it altogether. Its primary function of saving the court's time is already adequately catered for by the principle of exhaustion and, to some extent, also by the principle of *locus standi*. On the contrary, the decision-making process would be greatly simplified if the requirement of a *prima facie* view of an arguable case is replaced simply by a *prima facie* view of the sufficient interest of the applicant. Bearing in mind that the objective of the requirement for leave is not to place unnecessary obstacles in the way of the applicant, this approach would be consistent with Order 16.

On the other hand, if the principle of an arguable case is to be retained as a relevant matter for the exercise of the court's discretion, then it is important that every effort be made to streamline its meaning to ensure that it is uniformly applied. In this case, the preferred meaning should be evidence of substantive legal issues that merit judicial determination. In this sense, in the interest of consistency and uniformity, it should then be mandatory for the courts to apply it in all applications for leave. The weight attached to it should, however, be less than that attached to sufficient interest. Hence, it should be regarded only as a subsidiary or logically sufficient condition, and not a necessary one for the grant of leave. This means that, for example, if the court determines that an applicant has sufficient interest and yet finds that the application lacks an arguable case, the negative finding on this issue should not be an automatic bar to granting leave. Since the court's finding on the issue of an arguable case is only a provisional finding, based upon the limited evidence available to the court, and is subject to revisal later, the court should, after noting this finding, be free to proceed to consider other relevant legal principles. If at the substantive trial, however, no new evidence is adduced to support the application, then unless the trial judge forms a different opinion of the case, the finding of the court which heard the leave application would then be affirmed to avoid unnecessary argument of the case. The advantage of this approach is that, even though the applicant might lose the case, the satisfaction of knowing that the case was lost at the substantive level (on its merits) and not because of some technical rule that denies access to the court engenders more confidence in the judicial system.

In the order of priority, the next legal principle that should be considered by the court in deciding on leave is the principle of exhaustion. Apart from saving the court's valuable time, this principle is an important means of ensuring that judicial interference into the operations of administrative agencies is limited to only absolutely necessary occasions. It should, therefore, be mandatory for the courts to consider exhaustion in all applications for leave and made a necessary condition for the grant of leave.

Finally, in view of its relative importance, the principle of undue delay should be the last principle to be considered in an application for leave. Already, Order 16 Rule 4 makes its application optional, depending upon the discretion of the court. According to the Rule:

> (1) Subject to this Rule, where in any case the Court considers that there has been *undue delay* in making an application for judicial review or, in a case to which sub-rule (2) applies, the application for leave under Rule 3 is made after the relevant period has expired, *the Court may refuse to grant* --
> (a) *leave for the making of the application; or*
> (b) any relief sought on the application,
> if, in the opinion of the Court, the granting of the relief sought would be likely to cause *substantial hardship to, or substantially prejudice the rights of, any person or would be detrimental to good administration.*

This means that, unless the facts of an application show any evidence that there has been a delay in bringing the application, the court may, in the exercise of its discretion, opt not to consider the criterion at all. Notwithstanding the discretion of the court, if, on the other hand, the facts of an application indicate that there has been a delay in instituting the application and the court, for whatever reason, omits consideration of the issue, then the decision on leave is subject to an appeal on the grounds of failure to consider the principle of undue delay. In order to avoid unnecessary appeals on the issue, and also in the interest of uniformity, it is, therefore, desirable that it should be mandatory for the courts to consider it in all applications for leave. The impact of the court's finding on the decision on leave should, however, remain as it presently is. This means that the principle should be considered as a necessary condition for the grant of leave so that, unless the court's view on the issue is favourable to the applicant, leave should not be granted.

This proposed order of applying the relevant legal principles is illustrated in the table on the next page.

LEAVE DECISION TREE

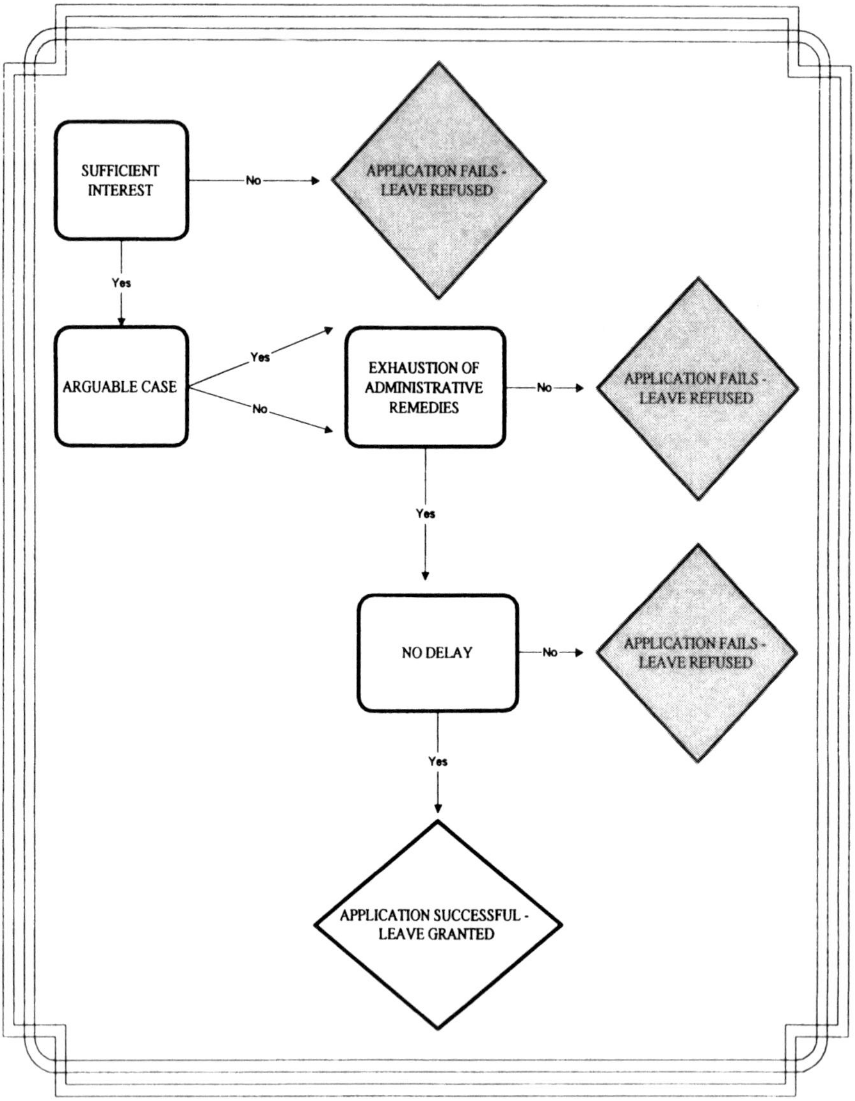

In order to reduce the chances of importing any irrelevant matters into the decision-making process, it may be quite useful to insert a checklist of the relevant matters in the order and manner proposed in every case-file. (See table of Checklist for Order on Leave on the next page). Judges should then be required to tick the items on the list to indicate the reasons for granting or refusing leave. Apart from ensuring that the relevant criteria are systematically and uniformly applied, the checklist will also go a long way in enhancing the system of keeping records at the National Court Registry.

CHECKLIST FOR ORDER ON LEAVE

1. Applicant has sufficient interest	☐ Yes	☐ No
	☐ Legal interest	☐ Busybody
	☐ Equitable interest	☐ Trivial complaint
	☐ Proprietary interest	☐ Frivolous or nuisance suit
	☐ Commercial interest	
	☐ Financial interest	
	☐ Economic interest	
	☐ Political interest	
	☐ Other interest	
2. Applicant has an arguable case	☐ Yes	☐ No
	☐ Constitutional issue	☐ Factual issue
	☐ Statutory interpretation	☐ Scientific/technical matter
3. Applicant has exhausted all administrative remedies	☐ Yes	☐ No
	☐ Statutory appeal exhausted	☐ Decision subject to statutory appeal
4. Application was instituted promptly	☐ Yes	☐ No
	☐ No delay	☐ Undue delay
5. If there is undue delay ...		
(a) Relief sought not likely to cause hardship to any person	☐ Yes	☐ No
(b) Relief sought not likely to prejudice any person's rights	☐ Yes	☐ No
(c) Relief sought not detrimental to good administration	☐ Yes	☐ No
6. Leave granted	☐ Yes	☐ No

Effect of Granting Leave

In deciding on leave, the court may exercise its discretion to grant or refuse leave. If it refuses leave, the applicant may appeal the decision to the Supreme Court. The procedure for appealing is examined in Chapter 12. If, on the other hand, the court exercises its discretion to grant leave, the decision, whether written or unwritten,[9] is usually given in the form of an order granting leave. Basically, when the court grants leave, it amounts to giving permission to the applicant to institute proceedings for the substantive hearing of the application for judicial review. By itself, the order granting leave implies nothing more and provides no other relief apart from that permission. If, however, the relief sought is an order of prohibition or *certiorari*, then the court may, under Rule 3(8)(a) of Order 16, direct that the order granting leave shall act as a stay of the proceedings to which the application relates until a determination of the substantive hearing or until a further order is made.

Summary Relief

Order 16 of the *National Court Rules* (Ch 38) makes no provision for summary relief. Hence, when a court makes an order granting leave, it cannot, strictly speaking, make an order summarily disposing of the substantive application. Some judges, as indicated above, have, however, occasionally disposed of judicial review cases in one fell swoop of the leave application. This was done by considering the substantive issues of the application during the leave proceedings under the issue of an arguable case.[10] The adoption of this approach, which has its merit under certain circumstances, has the same effect as making a peremptory order.

In England, where the position of the law on this point is the same as in Papua New Guinea, it is now conceded that the limitation imposed by

---

[9] Many of the National Court's decisions on leave remain unwritten judgments.

[10] From personal discussions with some of the judges who adopt this approach, it came to light that they were not unaware of the procedural irregularity of such an approach. They, however, justified their deviation from procedure on the ground of pragmatism and the exigencies of running a court trial in the provinces.

Order 16 on making peremptory orders during leave applications is inadvertent and, therefore, needs to be reformed. Taking into account the fact that the practice in Papua New Guinea, whether procedurally regular or not, already incorporates peremptory orders at the leave stage, it is necessary to amend the *National Court Rules*(Ch 38) to officially sanction the practice, for the courts cannot develop an underlying law of practice and procedure or formulate rules to fill gaps. *The National Court Rules* form a code of pleading practice and procedure which may be used as a guide in deciding matters of practice and procedure. The power to alter such rules, though given to the judges, is subject to the overriding sanction of Parliament.[11]

Interim Relief

If relief other than prohibition or *certiorari* is sought in an application for leave, the court may, under Rule 3(8)(b) of Order 16, grant any interim relief as could be granted in an action begun by writ. The obvious form of interim relief thus available is an interim injunctive relief. In granting such relief, the courts have always insisted on the application of the normal rules for obtaining an injunction. The relevant principles for obtaining an injunction, as laid down in *Employers Federation of PNG v PNG Waterside and Seamen's Union*,[12] are the following:

1. Is the action not frivolous or vexatious? Is there a serious question to be tried? Is there a real prospect that the applicant will succeed in the claim for an injunction at the trial?
2. The Court must then consider whether the balance of convenience lies in favour of granting or refusing interlocutory relief.
3. As to the balance of convenience the Court should first consider whether if the applicant succeeds, he would be adequately compensated by damages for the loss sustained between the application and the trial, in which case no interlocutory injunction should normally be granted.

---

[11] Ref. section 184 of the *Constitution*. See also, *South Pacific Post Pty Ltd v Nwokolo* [1984] PNGLR 38.

[12] (1982) N393.

4. If damages would not provide an adequate remedy, the Court should then consider whether if the applicant fails, the defendant would be adequately compensated under the applicant's undertaking in damages, in which case there should be no reasons on this ground to refuse an interlocutory injunction.
5. Then as one goes on to consider all other matters relevant to the balance of convenience, an important factor in the balance should, other things being even, preserve the *status quo*.
6. When all other things are equal, it may be proper to take into account in tipping the balance the relative strength of each party's case as revealed by the evidence before the Court hearing the interlocutory application.[13]

Granting Leave on Terms

Under Rule 3(7) of Order 16, the National Court may grant leave on such terms as to costs and as to giving security as it thinks fit. Usually, the Court grants leave without making any order as to costs or security. Indeed, in a case where the defendants attempted to intervene in an application for leave, the Court still declined to make any order as to costs, even though the application was unsuccessful. In this instance, the Court ruled that it was an error to serve notice of the application on the defendants.[14]

---

[13] *Id.*, p. 4.
[14] Ref. *Manjin v PTC*, above, note 3.

CHAPTER 12

APPEALS FROM THE NATIONAL COURT

Appeal Against the Decision on Leave

Order 16 of the *National Court Rules* (Ch 38) permits an appeal to the Supreme Court against the decision of the National Court to grant or to refuse an application for leave. Rule 11 says:

> An appeal by way of motion under Order 10 of the Supreme Court Rules to the Supreme Court may be made to set aside or discharge any order of the Court or a Judge granting or refusing an application for leave under Rule 3 or an application for judicial review.[1]

This provision, presumably, suggests that if for any reason leave is granted or refused, the applicant or the respondent may appeal the decision of the National Court to the Supreme Court, which may set aside the order granting or refusing the application for leave. Following from this, while a successful appeal by the applicant would result in the granting of leave, a successful appeal by the respondent would have the effect of refusing leave. On the other hand, in a reverse situation, while an unsuccessful appeal by the applicant means that leave is refused, an unsuccessful appeal by the respondent has the effect of granting leave. These possible scenarios of the impact of an appeal on the decision on leave, whether intended by Order 16 or not, raise a number of interesting questions. The first question is whether or not the recourse to appeal lies as a matter of right. If it does not, then is leave required in order to appeal? Secondly, who is the right party to bring an appeal? May the respondent also be permitted to appeal? If so, is it reasonable, in view of the *ex parte* nature of the proceedings from which the appeal lies, to permit such a course of action?

---

[1] Before the *National Court Rules* were amended by Practice Note of 28.8.85, there was no reference to Order 10 of the *Supreme Court Rules* in this Rule.

Is Appeal a Matter of Right?

The question as to whether the recourse to appeal provided for in Rule 11 lies as a matter of right or not was raised in *Ombudsman Commission v Donohoe.*[2] This question arose because, as a preliminary issue, counsel for the appellant submitted that the order of the National Court granting leave to the applicant to apply for judicial review of the proceedings of the Ombudsman Commission was not an interlocutory judgment but a final order. Accordingly, he argued that no leave was required pursuant to section 14(3) of the *Supreme Court Act* (Ch 37) in order to appeal to the Supreme Court. According to him, that appeal lay as of right pursuant to Rule 11 of Order 16 and section 4 of the *Supreme Court Act.*

The Supreme Court allowed the appeal but reserved its ruling on the question as to whether the appeal lay as of right or by way of leave. According to Pratt J, a pending amendment to the *Supreme Court Act*, which was due to come into force soon, would incorporate a special provision under Order 10 to accommodate appeals from orders concerning judicial review. Consequently, the jurisdictional problems posed by this case should not occur again in the future. Hence, the Court's decision not to rule on the question.

The anticipated amendment came into force on 1 February 1985. Under the amendment, Order 10 of the *Rules of the Supreme Court of Justice* lays down the procedure for appealing the decision of the National Court on leave. This Order, which supplements Rule 11 of Order 16 of the *National Court Rules*, provides as follows:

> ORDER 10 - APPEAL FROM ORDERS MADE UNDER ORDERS 16 AND 17 OF THE NATIONAL COURT RULES
>
> *DIVISION 1 - INSTITUTION OF APPEAL*
>
> 1. An appeal under this Part shall be instituted by a notice of motion.
> 2. The notice of motion and all subsequent proceedings shall be entitled 'In the Supreme Court of Justice' and shall be entitled between the party as appellant and the party as respondent.
> 3. The notice of motion shall -

[2] [1985] PNGLR 348.

(a) show where appropriate the particulars set out in a notice of appeal under Order 7 Rule 8;

(b) have annexed -

(i) copies of all documents which were before the Judge of the National Court appealed from,

(ii) a copy of the order made, certified by the Judge's Associate or the Registrar.

(c) be in accordance with form 15;

(d) be signed by the appellant or his lawyer; and

(e) be filed in the registry.

DIVISION 2 - CERTAIN RULES TO APPLY

4. The following rules shall apply to matters under this part with regard to -

(a) filing and service; Order 7 Division 4;

(b) affidavits; Order 7 Rules 61, 62, 63, 64.

The relevant provisions relating to notice of appeal under Rule 8 of Order 7 of the *Rules of the Supreme Court of Justice* provide, among other things, that the notice of appeal shall:

(a) state that an appeal lies without leave or that leave has been granted and or annex the appropriate order to the notice of appeal; ... [and]

(e) be in accordance with form 8.

Beyond this direction to state that an appeal lies without leave or that leave has been granted, the new rules provide no other guide on the procedure for appealing the decision of the National Court on leave. The question as to whether an appeal to the Supreme Court lies with or without leave, therefore, is still open.

In the absence of any rule or guide on the matter in the amendments introduced by Order 10 of the *Rules of the Supreme Court of Justice,* it appears that, like counsel for the appellant in the Ombudsman case, we are forced back onto the *Supreme Court Act* (Ch 37). The general provisions of this Act relating to the right of appeal from the National Court seem to be the most pertinent and, therefore, the starting point for discussion of the issue. These provisions state as follows:

PART III. - APPEALS TO THE SUPREME COURT

Division 1. - General

4. Right of Appeal from National Court.

(1) An appeal in accordance with this Act lies to the Supreme Court from a judgement of the National Court.

(2) An appeal lies in any civil or criminal proceedings, to the Supreme Court from a Judge of the National Court sitting on appeal -
(a) on a question of law; or
(b) on a question of mixed fact and law; or
(c) with leave of the Supreme Court, on a question of fact.

According to these provisions, the question as to whether an appeal against the decision of the National Court on leave lies as of right or by way of leave depends upon whether the grounds of the appeal involve a question of law, mixed fact and law or only a question of fact. As stated in the provisions, except in an appeal involving only a question of fact (in which case leave must first be obtained from the Supreme Court), appeals involving a question of law or mixed fact and law lie as of right and, therefore, do not require any leave.

In the Ombudsman case, Pratt J was sceptical of the relevance of this section of the *Supreme Court Act.* As he stated:

> Mr Colquhoun-Kerr for the appellant has placed his appeal on the alternate basis of appeal as of right under the *Supreme Court Act,* s 4, and appeal by leave under s 14. Personally I remain to be convinced of the relevance of s 4. It lays down appeal rights in very broad terms and must be read subject to later sections which spell out the factors distinguishing an appeal as of right and an appeal by way of leave. Sections 14 and 22 are especially pertinent.[3]

Indeed, section 14 of the Act, which governs civil appeals to the Supreme Court, using the same terms as section 4, also makes a question of law, mixed fact and law or only a question of fact the distinguishing factors of an appeal as of right or an appeal by way of leave.[4] However, in this case, these factors are qualified in the following terms:

(3) No appeal lies to the Supreme Court without leave of the Supreme Court -
...
(b) from an interlocutory judgement made or given by the National Court except -
...
(iii)in such other cases prescribed by the Rules of Court as are in the nature of final decisions;..

In relation to an appeal against the decision of the National Court under Order 16, these provisions mean that unless the order by the

---

[3] *Id.*, p. 350.

[4] Ref. section 14(1) of the *Supreme Court Act* (Ch 37).

National Court is regarded as a final decision, an appeal against it would lie only by way of leave of the Supreme Court. In the Ombudsman case, counsel for the appellant invited the Court to treat the order of the National Court as one "in the nature of a final decision" under section 14 (3)(b)(iii) of the *Supreme Court Act.* Pratt J, with Amet J (as he then was) concurring, reluctantly went along with this submission but pointed out that:

> I am also unimpressed with the submission that the National Court order may be treated as a final order and not an interlocutory one. True it is that a person who is unsuccessful in his application for review has a final order (subject to appeal), but on the other hand if the applicant is successful it is really the second step in an ongoing process. The situation seems to be reminiscent of the old *Rules of the Supreme Court* (UK), O 25, r 3, dismissing an action on a point of law where it was held that such dismissal was not final because had the decision gone the other way, the action would have proceeded: *Salaman v Warner* [1981] 1 QB 734 applying the test laid down by Brett LJ in *Standard Discount Co v La Grange* (1877) 3 CPD 67.
> Although I am far from totally convinced of the applicability of the *Supreme Court Act*, s 14(3), in circumstances such as the present, the matter is at least arguable and I would propose the granting of leave but in the ultimate dismiss the appeal.[5]

Notwithstanding the fact that Order 16 of the *National Court Rules* (Ch 38) makes no provision for summary relief, the ruling of Pratt J on the issue is appropriate in the circumstances, as it accords with the status of the National Court. The National Court being a court of superior jurisdiction, it is most appropriate in the particular circumstances of Papua New Guinea to treat its orders as one "in the nature of a final decision". This is because it exercises powers, particularly the power of judicial review, which are equivalent to those conferred on the High Court in the U.K. An order, such as declaratory order, *mandamus*, *certiorari*, prohibition, with the possible exception of an injunction, which may be interlocutory, issuing from the High Court (U.K.), unless prescribed by the Rules of Court to be otherwise, is normally treated as one in the nature of a final decision. This is more so because the orders are dispositive of the issues before the court hearing the application, and it is the finality of the order that subjects it to appeal to a higher court.

---

[5] Above, note 2 at 350.

On the question of the applicability of section 14(3) of the *Supreme Court Act*, notwithstanding His Honour's doubts, all indications point to the applicability of the section. In the first place, section 14 comes under Division 2 of the Act, which is entitled "Additional Provisions Relating to Appeals in Civil Cases". Section 13 of the Act, which explains the application of the Division, expressly states that "This Division applies to and in relation to proceedings other than criminal proceedings". Secondly, section 14 itself is subtitled "Civil Appeals to the Supreme Court". The labels of these headings are by themselves significant in that they suggest that, apart from the general provisions of section 4 of the Act relating to appeals to the Supreme Court, the question as to whether an appeal lies to the Supreme Court as of right or by way of leave further depends upon whether the case is a civil or criminal appeal. Now, since the Ombudsman case was a civil appeal to the Supreme Court, this brings it squarely within the ambit of section 14 of the Act, which stipulates the relevant provisions governing the procedure for civil appeals. In the particular circumstances of the Ombudsman case, therefore, there is no doubt about the applicability of section 14(3) of the *Supreme Court Act*.

Ipso facto, if, on the other hand, the case had been a criminal appeal, then, in addition to the general provisions of section 4 of the Act relating to appeals to the Supreme Court, the question as to whether an appeal lies to the Supreme Court as of right or by way of leave would then have to be resolved by reference to section 22 of the Act. This section comes under Division 3 of the Act, entitled "Additional Provisions Relating to Appeals in Criminal Cases". According to the Act, "This Division applies to and in relation to criminal proceedings." The relevant provisions governing these proceedings state as follows:

> 22. Criminal Appeals.
>
> A person convicted by the National Court may appeal to the Supreme Court -
>
> (a) against his conviction, on any ground that involves a question of law alone; and
>
> (b) against his conviction, on a question of mixed fact and law; and
>
> (c) with the leave of the Supreme Court, or on the certificate of the National Court that it is a fit case for appeal, against his conviction on any ground of appeal -
>
> (i) that involves a question of fact alone; or

(ii) that appears to the Supreme Court to be a sufficient ground of appeal; and

(d) with the leave of the Supreme Court, against the sentence passed on his conviction, unless the sentence is one fixed by law.

Assuming that the current position of the law on determining the question as to whether an appeal against the decision of the National Court on leave lies as of right or by way of leave is as we have argued above, then the amendments introduced by Order 10 of the *Rules of the Supreme Court of Justice* leave much to be desired. Of course, since it is now clear that Order 10 of the *Rules of the Supreme Court of Justice* and not Rule 11 of Order 16 of the *National Court Rules* is now the basis of appeal against the National Court decision on leave, the new Rules seem to have taken care of the jurisdictional problem that arose in the Ombudsman case.

However, notwithstanding the special provisions under the new Rules relating specifically to appeals from orders concerning judicial review, the question as to whether an appeal against the decision of the National Court on leave lies as of right or by way of leave, as demonstrated above, still has to be resolved by reference to the general provisions relating to the right of appeal from the National Court in the *Supreme Court Act*. Taking into account the numerous provisions from multiple rules and the various stages of complex analysis that one has to go through in order to determine this question, the situation as it presently exists is, to say the least, most unsatisfactory.

There are a number of possible ways to redress this situation. The first way is to repeal Order 10 of the *Rules of the Supreme Court of Justice* and allow appeals to be based upon Rule 11 of Order 16 of the *National Court Rules* as of right. The argument supporting this would be that even if Order 16 was silent on the question of appeal, the decision of the National Court to grant or refuse an application for leave would, nevertheless, be subject to appeal. This is so by reason of the fact that the Supreme Court has appellate jurisdiction to review all National Court decisions.[6] In this instance, the procedure for appealing would be determined according to the *Supreme Court Act*. In other words, a general right of appeal already exists which could be invoked by parties

---

[6] Ref. section 155(2) of the *Constitution*.

who are dissatisfied with the decision on leave. The fact that it is considered necessary to make specific provision in Order 16 for appealing against the decision on leave cannot be taken for granted. Among other things, it indicates a recognition of the distinct importance of the judicial review process, which justifies emphasising the availability of appeals against the National Court's exercise of discretion to grant or refuse an application for leave to apply for judicial review. In fact, this same rationale seems to underlie the introduction of the special provisions under Order 10 of the *Rules of the Supreme Court of Justice*, which inadvertently omitted to address the problem comprehensively enough. In furtherance of this rationale, it is arguable that Rule 11 of Order 16 of the *National Court Rules* intended to facilitate the procedure for appealing to the Supreme Court, and it did this by specifying a procedure that notably omits any reference to the requirement for leave.

Further support for allowing appeals to be based upon Rule 11 of Order 16 of the *National Court Rules* as of right may be derived from the fact that there already exists a requirement that an applicant for judicial review must first obtain leave from the National Court. This is a major hurdle that all applicants must first clear in order to be allowed to invoke the judicial review jurisdiction of the court. To require an applicant to obtain another leave in order to appeal puts an unnecessary burden on the applicant and further complicates the judicial review procedure. Once again, it is important to be mindful of the objective of Order 16, which is to simplify the judicial review process and not to further complicate it. Any procedure or interpretation of the Rules that would be inconsistent with the objectives of Order 16 should, therefore, be discouraged.

In the Ombudsman case, Pratt J flatly rejected the submission that appeal lay as of right, pursuant to Rule 11 of Order 16 of the *National Court Rules*, because "[t]he National Court judges cannot of course lay down methods of procedure to be followed by the Supreme Court".[7] Dismissing the relevance of Rule 11 of Order 16 of the *National Court Rules,* he explained that this particular rule was brought into effect in anticipation of the *Rules of the Supreme Court of Justice* and was, therefore, supposed to be keyed in with sections 4 and 14 of the *Supreme Court Act*. According to him, this did not happen as planned and,

[7] Above, note 2 at 350.

instead, the Rules were completely redrafted to incorporate a special provision under Order 10 of the *Rules of the Supreme Court of Justice*. Looking back at the Ombudsman case now with help of hindsight, it is ironical to recall that one of the reasons why His Honour reserved his ruling on the question as to whether the appeal lay as of right or by way of leave was because he had hoped rather optimistically that "[w]ith the introduction of the new *Supreme Court Rules* this year the question will now be of academic interest only".[8] Unfortunately, this hope, as the turn of events has sadly shown, has not materialised.

From the general tenor of all the provisions of the *Supreme Court Act* regarding appeals to the Supreme Court, there seems to emerge a trend that appeals to the Supreme Court on grounds involving a question of law or mixed fact and law, with the possible exception of appeals from criminal proceedings, should be regarded as a matter of right. If that is the case, then another possible way to redress the present situation regarding appeals from orders made under Order 16 of the *National Court Rules* is to amend Order 10 of the *Rules of the Supreme Court of Justice* so that all appeals from orders made under Order 16 of the *National Court Rules* would lie automatically as a matter of right. This approach would be justified by the fact that there already exist built-in mechanisms in the application for leave procedure that ensure that only questions of law are considered at the leave stage of applying for judicial review.

The first of these mechanisms is the principle of an arguable case. This principle, as explained above, requires that before leave is granted, an application for leave to apply for judicial review must raise substantive legal issues that merit judicial determination. If this principle is correctly and consistently applied, an appeal against the decision on leave to the Supreme Court would then have to be necessarily restricted to only the legal issues which the trial court is required to take into account in granting or refusing leave. Hence, if the appeal is allowed as a matter of right, it would not only simplify the procedure and save costs and time but it would also be consistent with the objective of the *Supreme Court Act*, which is to regard, as a matter of right, all appeals to the Supreme Court on grounds of appeal involving a question of law.

[8] *Ibid.*

Another built-in mechanism in the application for leave procedure that should necessarily restrict an appeal from orders made under Order 16 of the *National Court Rules* to only questions of law is the relevant criteria for making a decision on leave. As explained above, the only relevant matters for the exercise of the court's discretion on granting or refusing leave are the sufficient interest of the applicant, evidence of an arguable case, exhaustion of all available administrative remedies and the time limit for instituting the application. All these matters are legal issues based upon legal principles. Hence, as long as these issues are correctly and consistently considered by the trial court, then any appeal against the decision on leave cannot but be based upon the grounds that necessarily relate to the relevant matters for the court's exercise of discretion and how the relevant principles were applied. This inevitably should restrict the appeal to only questions of law and, thus, justify allowing the appeal as of right.

Who is the Right Party to Bring an Appeal?

Even if the question of whether an appeal to the Supreme Court from the decision of the National Court on leave to apply for judicial review lies as of right or by way of leave is resolved, there remain fundamental questions about the procedure for appealing the decision on leave. Rule 11 of Order 16 of the *National Court Rules* simply states that "An appeal ... to the Supreme Court may be made to set aside or discharge any order of the Court or a judge granting or refusing an application for leave under Rule 3 ..." This raises a fundamental question as to who is the right party to make such an appeal. Is it the applicant for leave or the respondent, or both of them?

This question arises because, according to Rule 3(3) of Order 16 of the *National Court Rules,* it is only the Secretary for Justice who is required to be notified of an application for leave. In practice, this means that it is only the Secretary for Justice who, on behalf of the State, may be permitted to make an appearance during an application for leave. Furthermore, since the application for leave is required to be heard *ex parte*, the respondent, who is not required to be notified nor served, is not expected to participate in the leave proceedings.[9] Hence, except for the Secretary for Justice, it is theoretically not possible for a respondent to be even aware of the fact that an application has been filed. Indeed, if the application for leave fails, the respondent, theoretically, would never have the chance of hearing about it. The first opportunity that the respondent has to ever hear about the application is after leave is granted. At this stage, the summons which is required to be served on the respondent relates to the application for judicial review and not the application for leave.

In these circumstances, it is logical and quite reasonable to assume that only the applicant for leave may be permitted to appeal against the National Court decision on leave. Yet this assumption is not borne out by the rules of procedure governing an appeal to the Supreme Court nor by practice in the courts. In Order 10 of the *Rules of the Supreme Court of Justice,* the only reference to the parties to an appeal from orders made under Order 16 of the *National Court Rules,* is that "[t]he notice of motion and all subsequent proceedings shall be entitled ... between the party as appellant and the party as respondent".[10] As to who the parties should be, there is no further direction. The *Supreme Court Act* is not of much help either on the issue. Apart from section 22 of the Act, which clearly states that "[a] person convicted by the National Court may appeal to the Supreme Court ..." and, thereby, indicates the party intended, the other provisions offer no such guide. Section 4(2) of the Act simply states that "An appeal lies in any civil or criminal proceedings, to the Supreme Court from a Judge of the National Court ..." Similarly, section 14(1) of the Act states that "... an appeal lies to the Supreme Court from the National Court ..."

The general terms in which these provisions are expressed seem to suggest that both the applicant for leave and the respondent may appeal the National Court's decision on leave. If that is the intention of these rules, then it raises some logical problems regarding practice and procedure. Of course, as the party whose application is being considered, it is quite reasonable to expect that the applicant for leave would have a

[9] Ref. *Manjin v PTC* [1990] PNGLR 288, where the Court refused the defendant's request to intervene in the plaintiff's application for leave, the Court pointed out that it was an error for the applicant for leave to serve the respondent.
[10] Rule 2.

direct interest in the outcome of the application for leave which should be protected by law. It is, therefore, just and proper that provision be made for the applicant to appeal against the decision on leave. With regard to the respondents, however, while it is possible to argue that they may also have a stake in the outcome of the decision on leave, to permit an appeal by them clearly contradicts the procedure laid down by Order 16 of the *National Court Rules* for applying for leave.

In addition, from the provisions of Order 16 of the *National Court Rules*, it is quite evident that the law itself does not consider the respondent's interest in an application for leave on the same level as that of the applicant. This why the application for leave is determined by reference to the sufficient interest of the applicant and not the respondent. For the same reason, the application for leave to apply for judicial review is made an *ex parte* proceeding, precluding participation by the respondent. It is, thus, arguable that if the respondent's interest in the decision on leave were considered to be at par with that of the applicant, the law would have made provision for intervention in the process. If it is not considered necessary for the respondent to participate in the application for leave in the first place, then it is doubly difficult to justify allowing the respondent to appeal against the decision on leave.

The practice in the courts also defies the logic of restricting appeals against the National Court decision on leave to only the applicant for leave. The Ombudsman case established the precedent for allowing a respondent to appeal. In that case, the Supreme Court allowed the Ombudsman Commission, which was the respondent in the application for leave, to file an appeal against the decision on leave. Not surprisingly, right at the outset of the case, the issue arose as to how this matter came before the Supreme Court from an *ex parte* judgment. From the chronology of events it was revealed that:

> The order granting leave to apply for judicial review was made on 18 November 1983, and the originating summons to commence the application pursuant to the *National Court Rules* 1983, O 16, r 5 (the Rules) was filed on the same day. The notice setting the matter down for trial was filed on 21 November 1983 and notice of intention to defend was filed on 5 December 1983. On 22 December 1983 the defendant Ombudsman Commission filed the notice of appeal in this Court against the order granting leave to apply for judicial review. On 18 January 1984, the defendant then sought by motion, a stay of

> further action in the application for review until the disposition of this appeal. On 20 January 1984 an order to that effect was made by consent.[11]

This chronology of events raised obvious procedural questions regarding the propriety of the way the matter came before the Supreme Court. Notwithstanding this, the Court allowed the appeal to proceed without addressing the questions. In view of the novelty of permitting a respondent to an application for leave to file notice of appeal against the order granting leave to apply for judicial review, plus the additional fact that there was no appearance, either in person or by counsel, for the respondent (applicant for leave), perhaps a little clarification of the reasons that justify such permission might have been in order. But then, of course, in the absence of the respondent (applicant for leave), the Court was naturally denied the benefit of argument on the issue.

Under these circumstances, the grounds upon which the appeal may be based pose rather puzzling questions of procedure. These questions are all the more puzzling because an appeal, whether on a question of law, a question of mixed fact and law or on a question of fact, presumes that the grounds of the appeal would relate to the issues discussed by the trial court. Since the court is not required to hear arguments at the leave stage, the application being *ex parte*, no substantive legal issues are discussed at this stage of the proceedings. Of course, if an applicant for leave appeals against the decision on leave, it is reasonable to assume that the grounds of appeal would relate to the relevant matters for the court's exercise of discretion and how the relevant principles were applied. If, on the other hand, a respondent other than the State appeals, it is difficult to imagine any possible grounds that could lead to a successful appeal against the decision on leave. The reason being that since the respondent is deemed to have no information relating to the application for leave and cannot rely on any substantive legal issues because these were not before the trial court, there is hardly any ground that can be sustained by the respondent. Indeed, this conclusion is supported by the way and manner in which the Court handled the grounds of appeal in the Ombudsman case.

---

[11] Above, note 2 at 352.

The first ground of the appeal, which was the central issue of the appeal, stated that "the Judgment of the Learned Judge was wrong in law in that Section 24 of the *Organic Law on the Ombudsman Commission* expressly provides that no proceeding or decision of the Commission shall be reviewed, challenged, quashed, held bad for want of form or called into question in any court, except on the ground that it lacked jurisdiction".[12] Under the particular circumstances of this case, it may be conceded that the issue of the jurisdiction of the National Court was arguably a valid ground of appeal for the respondent. Within the broader framework of judicial review today, however, there is no doubt whatsoever that it is a forgone conclusion that any attempt, whether by statute or subordinate legislation, to oust the judicial review jurisdiction of the National Court is an exercise in futility. This outcome is guaranteed not only by the common law presumption of reviewability of all cases but also by the *Constitution*. It is, therefore, not surprising that the Court rejected this ground of appeal precisely on the basis of the *Constitution.* In very emphatic language that is reminiscent of the English House of Lords guarding the integrity of the courts, Amet J held that,

> Section 24 of the Organic Law is, in my conclusion inconsistent with the s 217(6) grant of jurisdiction and right. It cannot stand. It is invalid and unconstitutional and must be struck down. To the extent that the applicant in the court below seeks a review of the proceedings of the Commission in its inquiry, on the ground of excess of jurisdiction, the National Court does have jurisdiction, and the court below did not err in law.[13]

Ground 2 of the appeal stated that "the judgment of the Learned Judge was wrong in law in that Order 16 Rule 1(2) of the *National Court Rules* does not confer jurisdiction to make the declarations sought under the circumstances which obtain in this case".[14] The Supreme Court, anxious to seize the opportunity offered by this ground to clarify the legal implications of the constitutional provisions referred to, responded in some detail to the substantive legal arguments raised by this ground. The Court was, however, quick to point out the contradictions inherent in the

---

[12] *Ibid.*

[13] *Id.*, p. 359.

[14] *Id.*, pp. 359-360.

ground of appeal. According to the Court, the arguments raised by this ground are:

> ... substantive legal arguments which required careful examination of the legal application of the provisions of the Rules and the *Constitution* upon the facts on the substantive application. On an application for leave to file an application for judicial review, the Court need only be satisfied as to the requirements of O 16, rr 2, 3 and 5. The application, of course, is ex parte and so the Court does not have any other material contesting the application...[15]

On the basis of this, the Court dismissed the second ground of the appeal as well. The import of the Court's ruling on this ground was that if the arguments raised by the ground of appeal could not have been considered at the application for leave stage because of the inconsistency with the *ex parte* nature of the proceedings, then obviously there is no basis for relying upon them as a ground of appeal. This conclusion, compelled by the demands of logic and consistency of the law, signify the anomaly of allowing the respondent to an application for leave to appeal against the decision on leave. For any attempt by a respondent to appeal the decision on leave is inevitably bound to run into this intractable problem.

It may be recalled that, notwithstanding the Supreme Court ruling on this issue, some judges had permitted argument of the substantive legal issues at the leave stage. This practice, admittedly, contravenes the Order 16 rules governing the procedure for applying for leave and also contradicts the Supreme Court decision on the issue. Be that as it may, it could be argued that if argument of the substantive legal issues is permitted at the leave stage, whether it is in error or not, then why can such issues not be accepted as valid grounds of appeal? There is no judicial authority on the issue. However, in view of the fact that permitting argument at that stage of the proceedings is clearly an error of law, it is very doubtful if the Supreme Court would allow an appeal based upon substantive issues arising from the leave proceeding.

Ground 3 of the appeal stated that "[t]he Learned Judge erred in the exercise of his discretion to grant leave in that the granting of the relief sought by the respondent: (a) Would serve no utility or serve any practical purpose; and (b) Would not determine any rights of Respondent

---

15 *Id.*, p. 361.

in respect of his employment".[16] The issues raised by this ground were clearly mistaken. At best, they seem to be residual arguments which convey the desperate attempt of the appellant to sustain the appeal. Naturally, the Court rejected this ground also and held that "the relief sought by the respondent applicant would have utility, if granted in his favour, in relation to future prospects of employment and his reputation generally".[17] Dismissing the ground, the Court pointedly observed that,

> ... the fact that the relief sought may not have utility and would determine no immediate employment rights of the respondent, fades into insignificance against the wider fundamental issues of constitutional and natural justice, principles that have evolved from the grounds raised, which conceivably would have arisen when the application went substantively before the National Court.[18]

Indeed, as to whether the relief sought would have any utility or determine any immediate employment rights of the respondent are not relevant matters for the exercise of the court's discretion at the leave stage. They are factors which the court takes into account in exercising its discretion regarding the appropriateness of the relief sought during the substantive trial. So, once again, the appellant (respondent to the application for leave) would be faced with the same contradictory situation. If the issue of the utility of the relief sought was not considered at the leave stage nor was it the basis of the decision to grant leave, then, obviously, it lacks merit as a ground of appeal.

The last ground of the appeal was that "[t]he Learned Judge erred in the exercise of his discretion to grant leave in that the granting of relief after such undue delay by the respondent in bringing his application would be prejudicial to good administration".[19] This ground of appeal is, of course, a relevant matter for the exercise of the court's discretion at the leave stage. Being a matter solely for the court's consideration, however, there is naturally no argument on the issue. Nonetheless, it is quite reasonable for an applicant whose application is refused on the ground of undue delay to appeal the decision on leave on this ground. It is also quite conceivable that a respondent who thinks that the issue was not properly considered by the trial court may be allowed to raise an

---

[16] *Id.*, p. 367.
[17] *Ibid.*
[18] *Ibid.*
[19] *Ibid.*

objection on the point as a preliminary issue at the substantive hearing of the case. If, however, the respondent appeals on this ground to the Supreme Court, the appeal is inevitably bound to run into major procedural difficulties.

First, in view of the fact that the leave application is an *ex parte* proceeding, intervention by the respondent is not permitted. Furthermore, under the Rule 3(3) of Order 16, except for the Secretary for Justice, the applicant is not required to notify or serve any other person, including the respondent. Under these circumstances, the respondent in the Ombudsman case is deemed to have no notice of the application and, in fact, did not participate in the leave proceedings. It is, therefore, difficult to imagine how this ground of appeal can be substantiated if the evidence supporting the argument of undue delay is not available to the respondent. Finally, and more fundamentally, the fact that there was no argument on the issue would defeat the ground, as the matter was not before the trial court. For precisely these reasons, the Supreme Court dismissed the final ground of appeal and held that,

> Once again I find the submissions advanced in this ground unconvincing and I am not disposed to disturbing the exercise of discretion to grant relief. It is doubly difficult, when the basis for the challenge is on a question which was not argued, the application for leave being ex parte, and on the further ground that the relief being sought in the substantive application would be prejudicial to good administration. Whatever the merit of this submission, the application was ex parte and so it could only be fairly argued in the substantive application.[20]

In the end, the Supreme Court dismissed the entire appeal and upheld the National Court decision to grant leave to the respondent (applicant for leave). While agreeing *in toto* with the Supreme Court decision in this case, the decision falls short of considering the full implications of the failure of the appellant to successfully sustain any of the grounds of appeal. As the decision clearly indicated, apart from the jurisdictional issue, which also could not be sustained, all the other grounds of appeal were dismissed essentially because they ran contrary to the procedure for applying for leave laid down by Order 16 of the *National Court Rules*. Since the jurisdictional issue, as pointed out above, is also one that could

---

[20] *Id.*, pp. 367-368.

never be successfully sustained on appeal, the logical inference from the Supreme Court decision is that as long as the Order 16 procedure is consistently adhered to, it is virtually impossible for a respondent to an application for leave, other than the State, to successfully appeal the decision on leave. If this is so, then it follows logically that, since it is well nigh impossible to substantiate any grounds of appeal, there is no rational basis for allowing a respondent other than the State to appeal.

For entirely different reasons, an argument could be made for treating the State also in the same manner as any other respondent on the question of allowing an appeal from the decision on leave. Of course, there is no question that the State, unlike other respondents, is a rightfully interested party deserving to appeal the decision on leave. Neither is there any doubt that the State may not face any of the procedural obstacles that other respondents face in sustaining the grounds of appeal. Still, allowing the State to appeal the National Court decision on leave is superfluous and unnecessary. This view is based upon the fact that under the rules of procedure outlined by Order 16 of the *National Court Rules* for applying for leave, the Secretary for Justice is required to be notified of all applications for leave and to be served with all the relevant documents filed in the application. In addition, the Secretary for Justice may be permitted to intervene in the proceedings. As indicated earlier, the rational for requiring notice to be served on the Secretary for Justice is to enable the State to appear during the leave application and, if necessary, to oppose the grant of leave if the application relates to a matter affecting the interests of the State. Hence, the State already has an opportunity at the leave stage to oppose the grant of leave if it has any objections. To permit an appeal to oppose the grant of leave a second time over, again, serves no useful purpose. It simply duplicates and further complicates the judicial review procedure. An analysis of the decision in *Kekedo v Burns Philp (PNG)*[21] illustrates the point.

In that case, the Supreme Court allowed an appeal by the Secretary for the Department of Labour and Employment (i.e. the State) against the National Court decision to grant leave. The facts leading to the appeal show that the case arose out of an industrial dispute between Burns Philp (PNG) Ltd and the Burns Philp Citizen Staff Association. The

[21] [1988-89] PNGLR 122.

association alleged several general issues of unfair practices by the senior management of Ela Motors, a subsidiary of Burns Philp, which were reported to the appellant as Secretary for the Department of Labour and Employment. Subsequently, a departmental tripartite committee investigated the issues raised by the allegations and submitted its report to the appellant. Based upon the report, the appellant then notified Burns Philp of the cancellation of the work permits of the two respondent employees.

Under section 9(4) of the *Employment of Non-Citizens Act* (Ch 374), "Any person aggrieved by the cancellation of a work permit ... may, within 14 days of notification of cancellation, appeal to the Minister whose decision is final". The notice of the cancellation was dated 16 August 1988. On 19 August, the respondents applied for leave to apply for judicial review of the Secretary's decision and consequential restraining orders. These orders and leave were granted on 24 August. On 29 August 1988, the respondents lodged an appeal to the Minister pursuant to section 9(4) of the *Employment of Non-Citizens Act.*

The principal ground of the appeal was that the respondents (applicants for leave) had not exhausted the available statutory remedy of appeal to the Minister under section 9(4) of the *Employment of Non-Citizens Act* (Ch 374) before invoking the judicial review power of the National Court. Responding to this ground, the Court referred to the relevant principles governing the exercise of judicial review jurisdiction where there is an alternative remedy by way of appeal.

Kapi DCJ found that, in applying these principles to the present case, the respondents had failed to bring themselves within the exceptions to the rule. The Court also reasoned that the respondents' attempt to avail themselves of the statutory remedy of appeal to the Minister as a safeguard against losing the substantive application after obtaining leave to apply for judicial review was "misconceived and mischievous". Amet J (as he then was), in the strongest terms possible, denounced the respondents' action. According to him:

> I cannot imagine that an aggrieved litigant who elects the option of going directly to a superior court of law for redress, would then be permitted, if he were unsuccessful, to pursue the alternative remedy before an inferior court. It is even more improbable to impossible to then seek to go back to an administrative tribunal such as, in this case, to a Minister. There are hierarchies of tribunals, from administrative

> to judicial, and if an aggrieved party chooses to bypass a statutory administrative remedy to a superior court, he cannot then be permitted to go back to the administrative remedy with the subsequent rights of appeal to the same superior court should he be further unsuccessful. I find the proposition quite mischievous and without substance. It would be tantamount to an abuse of process, in my view, for this Court to countenance such a contemplated course. See *Rundle v Motor Vehicles Insurance (PNG) Trust* [1987] PNGLR 44.[22]

On the basis of these two reasons, the Court granted the appeal and set aside the order of the National Court granting leave.

Upon close analysis of this decision, it appears that the decision was largely influenced by the particularly sensitive matter of employment of non-citizens and the policy considerations pertaining to this subject matter. Be that as it may, one wonders about the propriety of the stated ground of appeal in the case. This is because, even though the ground of appeal relates to a relevant matter for the exercise of the National Court's discretion on leave, it is a matter only for the court's consideration. Hence, if the National Court fails to exercise its mind on the matter, the resulting legal issue is the validity of a decision by the National Court on leave reached without taking into account a relevant matter, namely, exhaustion of administrative remedies. Since the Supreme Court is not the trial court in this instance, the question as to whether the respondents had actually exhausted the available statutory administrative remedies or not is not one that should be determined by the Supreme Court. That is a matter for the trial court to determine. The ground of appeal, therefore, should have been that the trial judge erred in the exercise of discretion to grant leave in that the judge did not exercise his mind on the question of exhaustion, and not that the respondent had not exhausted the available statutory remedy, as was stated in the case. This conclusion may be inferred from the *dicta* of Kidu CJ and Woods J in *PNG v Kapal*,[23] which was quoted by Amet J in support of his judgment. After expounding the rule relating to the principle of exhaustion, they stated *inter alia* that:

> We consider that in this case the learned trial judge should have considered whether or not to exercise the Court's powers of judicial review. In view of what we have already said on the merits, the fact that the trial judge did not exercise his mind on this matter makes very

[22] *Id.*, p. 127.

[23] [1987] PNGLR 417.

> little difference. But in future, we consider that this threshold question be decided before the National Court invokes its judicial review jurisdiction.[24]

If this analysis is correct, then it means that it is the validity of the decision of the National Court granting leave that should be the ground of appeal. Consequently, the Supreme Court's displeasure with the respondents' conduct of attempting to bypass a statutory administrative remedy in the erroneous belief that they could still return to it if their application for judicial review failed, was misplaced and directed at the wrong issue. For since the appeal to the Minister was lodged five days after leave had been granted by the National Court, this action, even if "misconceived and mischievous", was subsequent to the decision on leave and, therefore, could not be said to affect the validity of the decision on leave. Assuming, however, that the Supreme Court was right in directing its displeasure at the respondent rather than the National Court, that still did not justify allowing the State to appeal. For a strong case could be made that this matter could equally be handled by the court that would hear the substantive application. In other words, the State could request the judge hearing the substantive application to take the respondents' conduct into account before granting the relief sought. The time and cost of the appeal would then have been saved without in any way prejudicing the rights of the State.

Leaving aside the question of the propriety of the stated ground of appeal, the State, which is permitted to appear and to intervene during the leave proceedings, could easily have raised the arguments of this ground of appeal at the leave stage. That is, if the Secretary for Justice made an appearance. From the facts of the case, there is no indication as to whether there was an appearance on behalf of the State or not. If the State was represented but chose not to raise any objection to the grant of leave, then there is no justification for allowing it to appeal the decision on leave. On the other hand, if the State was represented and did object to the grant of leave, and yet leave was granted over its objection, then this may justify allowing it to appeal the decision on leave. Parenthetically, it is in this circumstance that the issue as to whether the respondents had exhausted the available statutory administrative

---

[24] *Id.*, p. 422.

remedies or not could be a proper ground of appeal. But even in such a situation, since the judge granting leave would then have exercised his mind on the matter, which is all the trial judge is legally required to do, the resulting decision would have complied with the rules for invoking the judicial review jurisdiction of the National Court. Consequently, the decision to grant leave could only be ascribed to the discretion of the judge, which is not and should not be subject to appeal. Hence, even in the extreme circumstance that a decision on leave is reached over the objection of the State, it is still not necessary and, thus, does not justify allowing the State to appeal the decision on leave.

In conclusion, the present position of the law which permits both the applicant for leave as well as the respondent to appeal the decision on leave is unsatisfactory. To redress this situation, it is necessary, indeed imperative, that the law is reformed to restrict appeals from the National Court decision on leave to only the applicant for leave. This would not only be logical and consistent with the Order 16 rules of procedure governing an application for leave but also would save time and costs and go a long way in rationalising and simplifying the judicial review process.

Appendix 1

National Court Rules (Order 16)

ORDER 16 - APPLICATIONS FOR JUDICIAL REVIEW

1. Cases appropriate for application for judicial review (U.K. 53/1)

(1) An application for an order in the nature of *mandamus, prohibition, certiorari* or *quo warranto* shall be made by way of an application for judicial review in accordance with the provisions of the Order.

(2) An application for a declaration or an injunction may be made by way of an application for judicial review, and on such an application the Court may grant the declaration or injunction claimed if it considers that, having regard to --

(a) the nature of the matters in respect of which relief may be granted by way of an order of *mandamus*, prohibition or *certiorari*;

(b) the nature of the persons and bodies against whom relief may be granted by way of such an order; and

(c) all the circumstances of the case,

it would be just and convenient for the declaration or injunction to be granted on the application for judicial review.

2. Joinder of claims for relief (U.K. 53/2)

On an application for judicial review any relief under Rule 1 may be claimed as an alternative or in addition to any other relief so mentioned if it arises out of or relates to or is connected with the same matter.

3. Grant of leave to apply for judicial review (U.K. 53/3)

(1) An application for judicial review shall not be made unless the leave of the court has been obtained in accordance with this Rule.

(2) An application for leave must be made by originating summons *ex parte* to the Court, except in vacation when it may be made to a Judge in chambers, and must be supported --

(a) by a statement, setting out the name and description of the applicant, the relief sought and the grounds on which it is sought; and

(b) by affidavit, to be filed before the application is made, verifying the facts relied on.

(3) The applicant must give notice of the application to the Secretary for Justice not later than two days before the application is made and must at the same time lodge with the Secretary copies of the statement and every affidavit in support.

(4) Without prejudice to its powers under Order 8 Division 4, the Court hearing an application for leave may allow the applicant's statement to be amended, whether by specifying different or additional grounds or relief or otherwise, on such terms as it thinks fit.

(5) The Court shall not grant leave unless it considers that the applicant has a sufficient

interest in the matter to which the application relates.

(6) Where leave is sought to apply for an order of *certiorari* to remove for the purpose of its being quashed any judgment, order, conviction or other proceedings which is subject to appeal and a time is limited for the bringing of the appeal, the Court may adjourn the application for leave until the appeal is determined or the time for appealing has expired.

(7) If the Court grants leave, it may impose such terms as to costs and as to giving security as it thinks fit.

(8) Where leave to apply for judicial review is granted, then --

(a) if the relief sought is an order of prohibition or *certiorari* and the Court so directs, the grant shall operate as a stay of the proceedings to which the application relates until the determination of the application or until the Court otherwise orders; and

(b) if any other relief is sought, the Court may at any time grant in the proceedings such interim relief as could be granted in an action begun by writ.

4. Delay in applying for relief (U.K. 53/4)

(1) Subject to this Rule, where in any case the Court considers that there has been undue delay in making an application for judicial review or, in a case to which Sub-rule (2) applies, the application for leave under

Rule 3 is made after the relevant period has expired, the Court may refuse to grant --

(a) leave for the making of the application; or

(b) any relief sought on the application,

if, in the opinion of the Court, the granting of the relief sought would be likely to cause substantial hardship to, or substantially prejudice the rights of, any person or would be detrimental to good administration.

(2) In the case of an application for an order of *certiorari* to remove any judgement, order, conviction or other proceeding for the purpose of quashing it, the relevant period for the purpose of Sub-rule (1) is four months after the date of the proceeding.

(3) Sub-rule (1) is without prejudice to any statutory provision which has the effect of limiting the time within which an application for judicial review may be made.

5. Mode of applying for judicial review (U.K. 53/5) (Amended by Practice Note of 28.8.85)

(1) Subject to Sub-rule (2), when leave has been granted to make an application for judicial review, the application shall be made by notice of motion to the Court.

(2) The notice of motion must be served on all persons directly affected and where it relates to any proceedings in or before a court and the object of the application is either to compel the court or an officer of the court to do any act in relation to the proceedings or to quash them or any order made in them, the notice of motion must

also be served on the clerk or registrar of the court and, where any objection to the conduct of the Judge is to be made, on the Judge.

(3) Unless the court granting leave has otherwise directed, there must be at least 14 days between the service of the notice of motion and the day named in it for the hearing.

(4) Within 21 days after grant of leave, the notice of motion shall be allocated a date for hearing by the Registrar after consultation with the parties.

(5) An affidavit giving the names and addresses of, and the places and dates of service on, all persons who have been served with the notice of motion must be filed before the notice of motion is entered for hearing and, if any person who ought to be served under this Rule has not been served, the affidavit must state that fact and the reason for it; and the affidavit shall be before the Court on the hearing of the notice of motion.

(6) If on the hearing of the notice of motion the court is of opinion that any person who ought, whether under this Rule or otherwise, to have been served has not been served, the Court may adjourn the hearing on such terms (if any) as it may direct in order that the notice of motion may be served on that person.

6. Statements and affidavits (U.K. 53/6) (Amended by Practice Note of 28.8.85)

(1) Copies of the statement in support of an application for leave under Rule 3 must be served with the notice of motion and, subject to Sub-rule (2), no grounds shall be relied on or any relief sought at the hearing except the grounds and relief set out in the statement.

(2) The Court may on the hearing of the notice of motion allow the applicant to amend his statement, whether by specifying different or additional grounds for relief or otherwise, on such terms as it thinks fit and may allow further affidavits to be used if they deal with new matters arising out of an affidavit of any other party to the application.

(3) Where the applicant intends to ask to be allowed to amend his statement or to use further affidavits, he shall give notice of his intention and of any proposed amendment to every other party.

(4) Each party to the application must supply to every other party on demand and on payment of the proper charges copies of every affidavit which he proposes to use at the hearing, including, in the case of the applicant, the affidavit in support of the application for leave under Rule 3.

7. Claim for damages (U.K. 53/7)

(1) On an application for judicial review the Court may, subject to Sub-rule (2), award damages to the applicant if --

(a) he has included in the statement in support of his application for leave under Rule 3 a claim for damages arising from any matter to which the application relates; and

(b) the Court is satisfied that, if the claim had been made in an action begun by the applicant at the time of his application, he could have been awarded damages.

(2) Order 8, Division 2, shall apply to a statement relating to a claim for damages as it applies to a pleading.

8. Application for discovery, interrogatories, cross-examination etc. (U.K. 53/8)

(1) Unless the Court otherwise directs, any interlocutory application in proceedings on an application for judicial review may be made to any Judge of the Court notwithstanding that the application for judicial review has been made and is to be heard by another Judge.

(2) In this sub-rule "interlocutory application" includes an application for an order under Order 9 Divisions 1 and 2, or Order 11 Division 3, or for an order dismissing the proceedings by consent of the parties.

(3) This Rule is without prejudice to any statutory provision or rule of law restricting the making of an order against the State.

9. Hearing of application for judicial review (U.K. 53/9) (Amended by Practice Note of 28.8.85)

(1) On the hearing of any summons under Rule 5, any person who desires to be heard in

opposition to the notice of motion, and appears to the Court to be a proper person to be heard, shall be heard, notwithstanding that he has not been served with the notice of motion.

(2) Where the relief sought is or includes an order of *certiorari* to remove any proceedings for the purpose of quashing them, the applicant may not question the validity of any order, warrant, commitment, conviction, inquisition or record unless before the hearing of the notice of motion he has lodged with the Secretary for Justice a copy verified by affidavit or accounts for his failure to do so to the satisfaction of the court hearing the notice of motion.

(3) Where an order of *certiorari* is made in any such case as is referred to in Sub-rule (2), the order shall, subject to Sub-rule (4), direct that the proceedings shall be quashed immediately on their removal to the Court.

(4) Where the relief sought is an order of *certiorari* and the Court is satisfied that there are grounds for quashing the decision to which the application relates, the Court may, in addition to quashing it, remit the matter to the court, tribunal or authority concerned with a direction to reconsider it and reach a decision in accordance with the findings of the Court.

(5) Where the relief sought is a declaration, an injunction or damages and the Court considers that it should not be granted on an application for judicial review but might have been granted if it had been sought in an action begun by writ by the applicant at the time of making his application, the

Court may, instead of refusing the application, order the proceedings to continue as if they had been begun by writ.

10. Saving for person acting in obedience to mandamus (U.K. 53/10)

An action or proceeding shall not be begun or prosecuted against any person in respect of anything done in obedience to an order of *mandamus*.

11. Appeal (Amended by Practice Note of 28.8.85)

An appeal by way of motion under Order 10 of the *Supreme Court Rules* to the Supreme Court may be made to set aside or discharge any order of the Court or a Judge granting or refusing an application for leave under Rule 3 or an application for judicial review.

12. Service on the Secretary for Justice

Service on the Secretary for Justice may be effected by leaving the document at his office in the Department of Justice, with the person apparently occupying the position of personal secretary to that Secretary.

Appendix 2

Sample Notice of Application

IN THE NATIONAL COURT)
OF JUSTICE AT WAIGANI)
PAPUA NEW GUINEA)

OS NO. 126 OF 1995

IN THE APPLICATION OF JUDICIAL REVIEW

IN THE APPLICATION OF **ZOLA BALM**

AND:
JOHN BOSSMAN
- First Respondent -

AND:
THE STATE
- Second Respondent -

AND:
PETER LUSMAN, SAM GONO AND JIM SOA
- Third Respondents -

NOTICE OF APPLICATION FOR LEAVE
TO APPLY FOR JUDICIAL REVIEW

SPACUM & SHAM
Lawyers
Level Twelve, Pacific Place
Musgrave Street
P O Box 769
PORT MORESBY
Telephone: 329-1746
Facsimile: 329 9601

IN THE NATIONAL COURT)
OF JUSTICE AT WAIGANI) O.S. NO. 126 OF 1995
PAPUA NEW GUINEA)

IN THE APPLICATION OF JUDICIAL REVIEW

IN THE APPLICATION OF **ZOLA BALM**

AND:
JOHN BOSSMAN
- First Respondent -

AND:
THE STATE
- Second Respondent -

AND:
PETER LUSMAN, SAM GONO, AND JIM SOA
- Third Respondents -

NOTICE OF APPLICATION FOR LEAVE TO APPLY FOR JUDICIAL REVIEW

To: The Secretary for Justice
Department of Attorney General
P. O. Wards Strip
WAIGANI.

The Applicant in the above matter hereby gives notice of *ex parte* application for leave pursuant to Order 16 Rule 3 of the *National Court Rules* to apply for judicial review.

Dated this 1st day of March 1995

Filed this 2nd day of March 1995

Appendix 3

Sample Originating Summons (Form 6)

IN THE NATIONAL COURT)
OF JUSTICE AT WAIGANI)
PAPUA NEW GUINEA)

OS NO. 126 OF 1995

ZOLA BALM
Plaintiff

JOHN BOSSMAN
First Defendant

THE STATE
Second Defendant

PETER LUSMAN, SAM GONO AND JIM SOA
Third Defendants

ORIGINATING SUMMONS

Dated : March 1995
Filed : March 1995

SPACUM & SHAM
Lawyers
P O Box 769
PORT MORESBY

Telephone: 329-1746
Facsimile: 329 9601
File Ref: 95/Z876:MAN:opp
Doc Name: jika/save.otml

IN THE NATIONAL COURT)
OF JUSTICE AT WAIGANI)
PAPUA NEW GUINEA) OS NO. 126 OF 1995

ZOLA BALM
Plaintiff

JOHN BOSSMAN
First Defendant

THE STATE
Second Defendant

PETER LUSMAN, SAM GONO AND JIM SOA
Third Defendants

ORIGINATING SUMMONS

The Plaintiff applies for:

1. Leave of the Court pursuant to Order 16 Rule 3 of the *National Court Rules* to apply for judicial review.
2. An Order in the nature of *Certiorari* to remove into this Honourable Court and quash the decision made on or about 10 February 1995 by the First and Third Defendants to cancel the entry permit of the Applicant and to order her removal from the country pursuant to sections 6 and 12 of the *Migration Act* (Ch 16).
3. An interlocutory Order restraining the Defendants and all their agents from the removal of the Applicant from Papua New Guinea pursuant to the removal order of 10 February 1995.
4. A Declaration that the said decisions of the First and Third Defendants were a denial of natural justice and that such decisions are accordingly null and void.
5. An Order in the nature of *Mandamus* or a mandatory injunction requiring the First Defendant to disclose and furnish to the

Applicant through her legal representative the grounds or reasons for the said decisions and order and be allowed to answer and make full representation to the Defendants.

6. Such further or other Orders as the Court deems fit.

Dated: 4th day of March 1995

Filed: 5th day of March 1995

Sam Dove of Spacum & Sham
Lawyer for the Plaintiff

Time and place for hearing:

Time:	6th March 1995 at 9.30 a.m.
Place:	National Court of Justice, Waigani
Applicant:	Zola Balm
Lawyers:	Spacum & Sham Level Twelve, Pacific Place, Musgrave Street, Port Moresby P O Box 769 Port Moresby) *Telephone:* 329-1746 *Facsimile*: 329 9601
Applicant's address for Service	Offices of Spacum & Sham Level Twelve, Pacific Place Musgrave Street, Port Moresby
Address of Registry:	National Court of Justice, Waigani National Capital District

Appendix 4

Sample Statement in Support

IN THE NATIONAL COURT)
OF JUSTICE AT WAIGANI)
PAPUA NEW GUINEA)

OS NO. 126 OF 1995

ZOLA BALM
Plaintiff

JOHN BOSSMAN
First Defendant

THE STATE
Second Defendant

PETER LUSMAN, SAM GONO, AND JIM SOA
Third Defendants

STATEMENT PURSUANT TO ORDER 16 RULE 3(2) OF THE NATIONAL COURT RULES

Dated: 4 March 1995
Filed: 5 March 1995

SPACUM & SHAM
Lawyers
P O Box 769
PORT MORESBY

Telephone: 329-1746
Facsimile: 329 9601

File Ref: jika/save.otml

IN THE NATIONAL COURT)
OF JUSTICE AT WAIGANI)
PAPUA NEW GUINEA) OS NO. 126 OF 1995

ZOLA BALM
Plaintiff

JOHN BOSSMAN
First Defendant

THE STATE
Second Defendant

PETER LUSMAN, SAM GONO AND JIM SOA
Third Defendants

STATEMENT PURSUANT TO ORDER 16 RULE 3(2) (a) OF THE NATIONAL COURT RULES

1. The name and description of the Applicant is Zola Balm, an Australian national, and holder of passport No. G 8563586 who is currently a lecturer in the Department of Law, University of Papua New Guinea.
2. Judgment, order, decision or other proceeding in respect of which relief is sought:
   (a) The decision of the First Defendant as Minister for Foreign Affairs made on or about 10 February 1995:
      (i) which purported to revoke the entry permit of the Applicant pursuant to section 7 of the *Migration Act* (Ch 16); and
      (ii) to issue a revocation notice to that effect.
   (b) The removal order made by the First Defendant as Minister for Foreign Affairs pursuant to section 7 of the *Migration Act* (Ch 16) on or about 10 February 1995 ordering that the Applicant be removed out of the country within 14 days of the date of the service of the order.

(c) The decision of the Third Defendants sitting as a Committee of Review pursuant to section 6(3) of the *Migration Act* (Ch 16) which decision upheld the Revocation of Entry Permit and Removal Order in respect of the Applicant made by the First Defendant on or about 10 February 1995.

2. Relief sought:

(i) A Declaration that the said decisions of the First and Third Defendants were unlawful acts within the meaning of section 37(11) of the *Constitution.*

(ii) A Declaration that the revocation of the Applicant's entry permit pursuant to section 7 of the *Migration Act* (Ch 16) with an accompanying threat of removal from the country is an unlawful act within the meaning of Sub-division C of Division 3 of Part III of the *Constitution.*

(iii) A Declaration that the said decision of the Third Defendants was an unlawful act within the meaning of section 41 of the *Constitution.*

(iv) A Declaration that the said decision of the Third Defendants was a denial of natural justice contrary to section 59 of the *Constitution* and is accordingly null and void.

(v) An Order of *Certiorari* quashing the decision and order of the First Defendant set out above.

(vi) An Order restraining the First Defendant and all his agents from taking any steps to enforce or attempt to enforce the revocation of the applicant's entry permit or the removal of the Applicant from Papua New Guinea.

(vii) An Order of Mandamus directed to the First Defendant requiring him to discharge his statutory duty under section 6 of the *Migration Act* (Ch 16) to disclose and furnish to the Applicant the grounds or reasons for the said decision and order.

3. Grounds:

(i) The Minister for Foreign Affairs, in revoking an entry permit of a non-citizen under section 7 of the *Migration Act* (Ch 16) and a Committee of Review appointed under that section to review the Minister's decision are deemed to be determining the existence or extent of a civil right and accordingly the proceedings should have been held in public in accordance with section 37(12) of the *Constitution* or, alternatively, if other persons were excluded pursuant to section 37(13) of the *Constitution*, then the Applicant should have been present during such proceedings.

(ii) The revocation of an entry permit pursuant to section 7 of the *Migration Act* (Ch 16) with an accompanying threat of removal from the country is an actual or imminent infringement of the qualified rights set out in Sub-division C of Division 3 of Part III of the *Constitution* and should accordingly comply with the provisions of section 38 of the *Constitution*.

(iii) The said decision of the Third Defendants pursuant to section 6(3) of the *Migration Act* (Ch 16) which upheld the Revocation of Entry Permit and Removal Order in respect of the Applicant was, contrary to section 41 of the *Constitution*, harsh, oppressive, not warranted by and disproportionate to the requirements of the Applicant's case and was otherwise not in the particular circumstances of the Applicant's case reasonably justifiable in a democratic society, having proper regard for the rights and dignity of mankind.

(iv) By section 59 of the *Constitution*, persons whose interests are affected by the decision of an authority, whether quasi-judicial, judicial, or administrative are required to be accorded the rules of natural justice.

(v) The Minister for Foreign Affairs is under a mandatory statutory duty to by virtue of section 6 of the *Migration Act* (Ch 16) to disclose and furnish to any persons whose entry permits are revoked and who are to be deported the grounds or reasons for the revocation and deportation orders.

(vi) On 11th February, 1995, the Applicant wrote to Mr. Tura requesting that her case be reviewed by a Committee of Review and setting out some eleven grounds upon which such request was made. The detail of these grounds are irrelevant except to say that the Applicant did claim that she had never been guilty of any misconduct leading to any complaint against her, she had never been prosecuted in any court of law either civilly or criminally, that she had not been given the opportunity of a fair trial and generally that the deportation notice violated the *Constitution*, in particular Pt. III, Div 3 (basic rights) and Div. 4 (principles of natural justice). The Applicant said she would be pleased to appear before the Committee of Review.

(vii) On 19th February, 1995, the Applicant wrote another lengthy letter to Mr. Tura speculating upon the possible reasons for the revocation and advancing many arguments against them. The detail of this letter is again irrelevant except to say that one of the matters raised was the Applicant's admitted comment on the Bougainville situation during a radio talk-back show in January 1995.

(viii) Under the *Migration Act* (Ch 16), a Committee of Review is appointed by the Prime Minister. On 20th February, 1995, Mr. G. H. Yaweb wrote a letter to the Applicant which (omitting formal parts) stated as follows:

'I write to advise you that the Committee of Review will consider your application on Tuesday, 26th February 1995 at 10.00 am at the Conference Room, 12th Floor, Bololo House, Waigani.

Any written statements from yourself or third persons which you may wish the Committee to consider should be submitted to Ms. Loko Nova of this Department prior to 4.06 p.m. on Monday, 25th February, as should any request to appear personally before the Committee.

I am instructed to advise you that the main reason for the revocation of your entry permit is that the Government will not allow non-citizens to remain in Papua New Guinea, who involve themselves in activities which it considers to be disruptive and detrimental to the good government of this country, and in particular, your unauthorized and provocative comments on the Bougainville situation during a radio talk-back show.'

(ix) On 21st February, 1995, the applicant wrote to Mr. G. H. Yaweb enclosing her letter of 19th February and requesting particulars of the allegations made in the third paragraph of her letter of 20th February. In addition the Applicant requested that she be given the opportunity of personally appearing before the Review Committee at the time and place appointed.

(x) On the 22nd February, 1995, Mr. G. H. Yaweb replied to the Applicant acknowledging receipt of her letter of 21st February and its contents. He stated that having considered the provisions of the *Migration Act* (Ch 16) there was no necessity for the Government to reply to a request for information.

(xi) The Applicant attended at the time and place fixed for the meeting of the Review Committee but was not allowed to appear personally before it. The Committee comprised the Minister for Commerce, Sir Peter Lusman, the Minister for Transport, Mr. Sam Gono and the Minister for Health, Mr. Jim Soa.

(xii) On 28th February, 1995, the decision of the Review Committee was communicated to the applicant by letter from Mr. Manu Pore, the Secretary for the Department of Foreign Affairs and Trade. The contents of the letter stated in full as follows:

'I have been instructed by the Minister for Foreign Affairs and Trade to advise you of the decision of the Committee of Review which met on 26th February 1995 to consider your application for a review of the Notice of Revocation of your entry permit.

The Committee of Review carefully considered your application and all submissions from other parties. After lengthy deliberation, the Committee decided to uphold the revocation of your entry permit. Whilst your competence as a constitutional lawyer was not questioned, the Committee was of the view that you interfered unduly in sensitive political matters outside of your particular expertise. Your role as a lecturer does not entitle you to make public comments on sensitive national issues that are likely to discredit the Government of Papua New Guinea or cause disaffection among the people of Papua New Guinea.

Therefore, in accordance with the Notice of Revocation of Entry Permit dated 10th February 1995, you are required to depart from Papua New Guinea on or before 6th March 1995.'

Dated: 4th day of March 1995

Sam Dove of Spacum & Sham

Lawyer for the Plaintiff

Appendix 5

Sample Order Granting Leave

IN THE NATIONAL COURT)
OF JUSTICE AT WAIGANI)
PAPUA NEW GUINEA)

OS NO. 126 OF 1995

ZOLA BALM
Plaintiff

JOHN BOSSMAN
First Defendant

THE STATE
Second Defendant

PETER LUSMAN, SAM GONO AND JIM SOA
Third Defendants

ORDER

Ordered : 6 March 1995
Entered : 8 March 1995

SPACUM & SHAM
Lawyers
P O Box 769
PORT MORESBY

Telephone: 329-1746
Facsimile: 329 9601
File Ref: 95/Z876:MAN:opp
Doc Name: jika/save.otml

IN THE NATIONAL COURT)
OF JUSTICE AT WAIGANI)
PAPUA NEW GUINEA) OS NO. 126 OF 1995

ZOLA BALM
Plaintiff

JOHN BOSSMAN
First Defendant

THE STATE
Second Defendant

PETER LUSMAN, SAM
GONO AND JIM SOA
Third Defendants

ORDER

The Court Orders that:

1. The Plaintiff is granted Leave of the Court pursuant to Order 16 Rule 3 of the *National Court Rules* to apply for judicial review of the decisions of the Minister for Foreign Affairs and Trade and the Committee of Review to cancel the entry permit of the Plaintiff and to order her removal from the country pursuant to section 6 and 12 of the *Migration Act* (Ch 16).
2. Until further Order, there be an Order restraining the Minister for Foreign Affairs and Trade and all his agents from the removal of the Plaintiff from Papua New Guinea pursuant to the removal order above.
3. There be liberty to apply on two days' notice.

Ordered: 6th day of March 1995
Entered: 8th day of March 1995

BY THE COURT

Appendix 6

Sample Notice of Motion

IN THE NATIONAL COURT)
OF JUSTICE AT WAIGANI)
PAPUA NEW GUINEA)

OS NO. 126 OF 1995

ZOLA BALM
Plaintiff

JOHN BOSSMAN
First Defendant

THE STATE
Second Defendant

PETER LUSMAN, SAM GONO AND JIM SOA
Third Defendants

NOTICE OF MOTION

Dated : 12 March 1995
Filed : 12 March 1995

SPACUM & SHAM
Lawyers
P O Box 769
PORT MORESBY

Telephone: 329-1746
Facsimile: 329 9601
File Ref: 95/Z876:MAN:opp
Doc Name: jika/save.otml

IN THE NATIONAL COURT)
OF JUSTICE AT WAIGANI)
PAPUA NEW GUINEA) OS NO. 126 OF 1995

ZOLA BALM
Plaintiff

JOHN BOSSMAN
First Defendant

THE STATE
Second Defendant

PETER LUSMAN, SAM
GONO AND JIM SOA
Third Defendants

NOTICE OF MOTION

Take notice that pursuant to the leave of the Honourable Ms Justice Sompo given on the 6th day of March 1995, the Court will be moved at 9.30 a.m. on the 15th day of March 1995 at Waigani for the following Orders:

1. An Order in the nature of *Certiorari* to remove into this Honourable Court and quash the decisions made on or about 10 February 1995 by the First and Third Defendants to cancel the entry permit of the Applicant and to order her removal from the country pursuant to sections 6 and 12 of the *Migration Act* (Ch 16).
2. An interlocutory Order restraining the Defendants and all their agents from the removal of the Applicant from Papua New Guinea pursuant to the removal order of 10 February 1995.
3. A Declaration that the said decisions of the First and Third Defendants were a denial of natural justice and that such decisions are accordingly null and void.

4. An Order in the nature of *Mandamus* or a mandatory injunction requiring the First Defendant to disclose and furnish to the Applicant through her legal representative the grounds or reasons for the said decision and order and be allowed to answer and make full representation to the Defendants.
5. Such further or other Orders as the Court deems fit.

AND the Plaintiff will seek an Order in respect of costs occasioned by this motion.

Dated: 12th day of March 1995

Filed: 12th day of March 1995

Sam Dove of Spacum & Sham
Lawyer for the Plaintiff

To: The Attorney General
Department of Attorney General
P. O. Wards Strip
WAIGANI.

To: The Minister for Foreign Affairs and Trade
Department of Foreign Affairs and Trade
P. O. Wards Strip
WAIGANI.

Index

CPSIA information can be obtained at www.ICGtesting.com
Printed in the USA
LVOW132359170612

286421LV00001B/2/P

9 789980 945860